designing with light
bars and restaurants

design

wi

designed by keith lovegrove

bars a

resta

ing
th light
nd
urants

jill entwistle

A RotoVision Book
Published and distributed by RotoVision SA
Rue du Bugnon 7
CH-1299 Crans-Près-Céligny
Switzerland

RotoVision SA, Sales & Production Office
Sheridan House, 112/116A Western Road
Hove, East Sussex BN3 1DD, UK

Tel: +44 (0) 1273 72 72 68
Fax: +44 (0) 1273 72 72 69
E-mail: sales@rotovision.com

Distributed to the trade in the United States by:
Watson-Guptill Publications
1515 Broadway
New York, NY 10036

10 9 8 7 6 5 4 3 2 1

ISBN 2-88046-434-X

Book design by Lovegrove Associates

Production and separations in Singapore by ProVision Pte. Ltd.

Tel: +65 334 7720
Fax: +65 334 7721

The author, editor and publisher would like to thank the following companies for their contributions to this book: Speirs and Major, Stiff + Trevillion, Kohn Shnier Architects, Claesson Koivisto Rune Arkitektkontor, Lighting Design International, Focus Lighting, Adam Tihany International, The Rockwell Group, Baynes and Co., Stoane Associated Architects, Mike Stoane Lighting, Paul Daly Design Studio, Hans Wolff and Partners, Claudio Lazzarini and Carl Pickering, Ulrike Brandi Licht, Ross De Alessi Lighting Design, Adams/Mohler Architects, Light Directions Limited, Absolute Action, Kevan Shaw Lighting, United Designers, Philips Lighting, Gradus Lighting, ETC, AC/DC.

Special thanks go to Dominic Meyrick of Marlin Lighting, Mary Rushton-Beales of Lighting Design House, Harry Barnitt of Zumtobel Lighting, David Kerr of Dynalite, Sally Storey of Lighting Design International, Miles Pinniger of Pinniger and Partners, Gerry Brown of Gebron Technical Services, Nick Kelso and Ted Glenny of Philips Lighting, Barry Hannaford of DPA Lighting Consultants.

A big thanks also to Mark Major of Speirs and Major.

Finally, a particular thank you to Keith Lovegrove for putting the words in a great design context and to editor Natalia Price-Cabrera for her patience and encouragement.

Jill Entwistle
London, 1999

Downlighting

 Uplighting

 Sidelighting

 Spotlighting

 Multi-directional lighting

 Backlighting

 Concealed lighting

 Special effects

 Daylight

 Narrow beam width

 Medium beam width

 Broad beam width

Alongside the images featured in this book, the symbols above describe the type of directional lighting used, with the beam widths as appropriate.
These symbols relate to the main lighting system in the relevant illustration.

contents

introd

section one

The British artist Patrick Caulfield has frequently found inspiring subject matter in the interior of a bar or restaurant. Invariably deserted, except perhaps for a solitary figure, the poignancy of the scenes he depicts lies in the very emptiness of spaces designed for conviviality. Light is often the only life – painfully exposing the tawdriness of a cheap mural with its fluorescence or casting its moon glow over a womb-like wine bar interior. The strange geometry of light and shade, reflection and shadow is one that Caulfield defines as integral to the bar and restaurant atmosphere.

Image

From the cliché of the candlelit supper to the discreet dichroics that lend their sparkle to the silver, lighting is an intrinsic ingredient of eating out. It establishes the image, the ambience, the marketing intention of a restaurant or bar. Should anyone need convincing of the crucial role which it plays in creating the appropriate atmosphere, consider the proposition of a romantic tryst in the bright, brash fluorescence of a burger joint.

Though light is playing its part there too, of course. The essence of a fast food outlet is to keep the punters moving. The cool, brilliant light patterns are part of the general interior message designed to discourage lingering.

Lighting not only illuminates an interior and its architectural elements, it is in itself an architectural element. It sculpts a space. At its most successful it adds another dimension to that space.

Imagine the transformation that takes place in the same interior in even the finest of establishments between first thing in the morning, as the waiters waft around polishing tableware, and the evening when the stage is set for dinner. From the dust-moted uniform light which dulls velvet and mutes crystal to the flickering candles which make the plush glow, the claret bottle glisten and the dark mahogany gleam. Lighting, as well as people, gives a restaurant soul.

The image of a bar or restaurant can be defined as much with lighting as with the decor in general. With the diversity of styles, cuisines and approaches from casual to funky to traditional to ethnic, it is less easy nowadays to gauge what to expect from a restaurant.

'Luigi's' in the old days might have conjured up faux grape-festooned trellis and candles in Chianti bottles, but what does Wagamama tell you? Now it is exterior impressions, interior design, lighting and the well-lit menu outside that convey the message.

'Lighting now becomes part of the theme that is the restaurant. It tells you the story that the name might not. When you look into the space you've got to have a picture being painted for you about the atmosphere,' says lighting designer Dominic Meyrick of Marlin Lighting.

In fact, Wagamama is a noodle bar, one of the first in a crop of new-style and stylish Japanese restaurants in the centre of London, and a good case in point. The emphasis here is on fast turnover, budget eating, with patrons all seated together at long refectory-style tables (although, of course, patrons are invariably sophisticated and relatively well-heeled). In such an atmosphere, the lighting scheme is not concerned with subtle patterning or architectural modelling.

'The lighting gives you the impression of canteenesque camaraderie and cheap food. It's quite bland, quite uniform and there's no highlighting as such,' says Meyrick. 'But it's still concealed, less in your face than, say, a fast food outlet.'

Sally Storey of Lighting Design International describes light as 'reinforcing the interior design statement of a restaurant' and believes that more and more interior designers and architects are recognising the contribution that the lighting specialist can make in exploring the potential of a concept. 'What I often find is that interior designers have got a particular idea and that I can take it beyond that with other alternatives that make the space

ting literally becomes part of the interior scheme at Coast, London, UK.
OGRAPH BY CHRISTOPHE KITCHERER.

The Spielboden in Dornbirn, Austria: light should both flatter and feel comfortable. PHOTOGRAPH © ZUMTOBEL LIGHTING.

People

work harder. That's what I think the lighting design skill is, that you can reinterpret the initial thoughts of the interior designer and make them more effective, by creating more effects than they thought possible with the lighting.'

This is perhaps particularly true of the larger, multiple purpose venue which is becoming increasingly prevalent in the family restaurant sector. Overall image and a sense of cohesion – as important a factor in the lighting as the interior scheme as a whole – are parallel considerations with creating individually appropriate atmospheres in, say, a video games area or a large eating space. In this context mapping out a lighting scheme is more problematic. A microcosm of that situation is also reflected in smaller restaurants which are now often required to fulfill more functions than in the past.

'Restaurants nowadays are often at least part bar, part restaurant so you want different atmospheres in different parts because people are wanting different things from that space. They might just want a drink, for instance, because they are there to meet people and not necessarily to eat. It's more complex,' says Dominic Meyrick.

What is crucial, therefore, is that like anywhere else, the lighting of restaurants and bars is considered at the very outset of a project, so that it is conceived and developed as an integral part of the interior. If the lighting cannot be properly integrated and positioned then the ideal effect is less likely to be achieved and the message may be mixed.

The social factor is clearly central to the whole experience of eating and drinking out. Lighting faces is therefore important. Whatever method is used, optimum illumination is achieved through balanced lighting from above and from the sides as it avoids hard shadows and visual monotony.

As well as ensuring that people are phsyiognomically flattered by the lighting, it is also important that their perception of the lighting is favourable. They must feel the lighting is conducive, comfortable and appropriate; they must be able to read the menu (here the age of patrons is a key consideration, as an older clientele will need higher light levels than a young crowd), and they must not be subjected to glare.

And lighting must make the space visually interesting. Visual monotony causes fatigue (one of the reasons why customers fail to hang around in the bright, uniform lighting of fast food outlets). With the correct lighting, the space becomes more textural, more interesting, more three dimensional.

According to lighting designer Sally Storey, this is where many restaurants and bars slip up. 'They tend to get the balance wrong – too much downlighting, for example, without thinking about the rest of it. The secret is to think about the lighting on different levels, to introduce variety and interest.'

Uniform lighting helps create a 'canteenesque camaraderie' at Wagamama, London, UK (overleaf).
COURTESY OF STIFF + TREVILLION (PREVIOUSLY KNOWN AS JSP ARCHITECTS). PHOTOGRAPH © MATTHEW WEINREB.

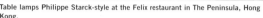

Table lamps Philippe Starck-style at the Felix restaurant in The Peninsula, Hong Kong.

UK pizza chain Pizza Express uses a tight spot on the table to create a candle effect. COURTESY OF LIGHT PROJECTS LTD. PHOTOGRAPH © TIMOTHY SOAR.

Philippe Starck uses uplighting to dramatic effect at the Teatriz in Madrid, Spain.

Techniques

Portable luminaires and pendants

Subdued lighting emanating from the table itself is a time-honoured part of the mix, and the candle is unlikely ever to be entirely extinguished. The circle of intimacy which is created by a pool of light in the centre is extraordinarily powerful, sensual and almost atavistic. The effect is often successfully mimicked with artificial light, primarily table lamps, though the drawback is that they can add clutter and where a restaurant has less than generously sized tables in order to fit in more customers, it may be impractical. They also mean that each table needs a power point unless the technique is restricted to those tables at the perimeter of the space (though battery operated table lights and candelabra are not uncommon in the US).

Miles Pinniger would nevertheless advocate them as a very effective approach. 'It's a lovely way of creating intimacy. You can have a very small table lamp – the footprint of the thing can be tiny. But you have to fix the thing into the table so it isn't either nickable or knockable.'

Glare-free pendant fittings suspended directly over the tables are another alternative, and somehow inextricably linked with the coffee shop ethos. From tiny contemporary Murano glass diffuser to industrial stainless steel helmet to 1970s' cotton mob cap, they go from retro to cutting edge. Their disadvantage, however, is that they are again lacking in flexibility if tables are likely to get moved around, and are not hugely successful either if they are hung at precisely the right height to obliterate the person sitting opposite.

Other options are to have luminaires at head height, perhaps mounted on adjacent partitions, or floor-standing, or affixed to walls. In all cases, the choice of diffuser (and source, of which more later) is pivotal. Lighting designers such as Sally Storey have their particular preferences.

'Very often I try to get luminaires with parchment shades, which is really good for soft lighting at the side [see Veeraswamy's, Section 2]. The effect you get from a table lamp in the living-room is more flattering than any downlighting will be on your face – so if I can introduce any lighting like that I will.'

Downlighting

'If you're looking for atmosphere then any ceiling-mounted fitting has got to be directional rather than anything diffuse,' maintains Miles Pinniger.

One of the most common strategies is to frame the table top with tightly directed light from recessed or surface-mounted ceiling fittings – small spots or directional downlights – which help create a sense of intimacy and define one table from another. However, the beam must be focused precisely. If it spills on to the heads of diners they will end up with less than flattering shadows down their faces. And bearing in mind that light will be reflected from the top on to faces, table or cloth colour has to be considered – yellow or green surfaces will leave patrons somewhat jaundiced.

Providing the beam is again kept very tight – usually eight to ten degrees – the same approach can also be used to mimic the effect of a centrally placed candle by directing it on to the table, a technique applied highly successfully by UK pizza chain Pizza Express for years using a Light Projects par 36 integral narrow beam spot. This pinspotting technique is only appropriate if the ceiling is not too high, however, otherwise it is impossible to focus the beam.

na Max restaurant, Hong Kong by Light Directions: foliage, which can also be ...anced with moving projections, offers tremendous potential for light and shadow ...cts. PHOTOGRAPH COURTESY OF LIGHT DIRECTIONS LTD.

Various techniques can be used to light artwork – here an accent spot with a soft edge to the beam is used. PHOTOGRAPH © ZUMTOBEL LIGHTING.

Park Hotel restaurant, Cardiff, Wales by DPA Lighting Consultants: linear xenon gives a warmer effect than fluorescent or cold cathode for cove lighting. PHOTOGRAPH BY NICK HOGGETT, DPA.

Uplighting

Uplighting fulfils a range of functions and is effective in that process of light layering which adds dimension to a space. It adds drama – uplighting columns or the base of a wall produces a theatrical and visually exciting result, for instance. When concealed behind a banquette – usually in linear form, perhaps gelled fluorescent or cold cathode – it can soften the area where the wall and ceiling planes meet and can have considerable impact with colour. It can create simple but striking effects for lighting walls, especially when combined with a downlit element.

The ways of achieving this form of indirect lighting are various – from buried floor fittings (ideal as a visual guidance system in passageways, for instance), floor-standing cylinders, wall mounted fittings and through concealed sources in covings and cornices.

Highlighting

The picking out of textures and tones, objects and architectural elements is a crucial part of a sophisticated lighting scheme. The light patterns which highlighting helps to weave create the visual interest which the human eye/mind enjoys.

Sculpture, paintings, flowers, foliage and objects that might be displayed in a theme restaurant or bar can all be brought to life with accent lighting. Again this can derive from recessed directional low voltage tungsten halogen downlights, surface-mounted spots or in the case of foliage, for instance, through discreet uplighting.

With artworks or textiles, exposure to ultraviolet light may cause fading so a UV filter may be necessary or lamps such as those made by Osram with UV stop quartz can be specified.

Coving and cornices are other details which provide an effective lighting opportunity. A subtle method of washing bands of the ceiling with soft light, the approach can vary according to the nature of the space – warm white light for a traditional upmarket restaurant, say, or coloured light for a more contemporary/sumptuous impression. Sources range from fluorescent, which can be sleeved in coloured gels, to cold cathode to xenon festoons.

'I'm very fond of the linear xenon lamp for use in cornices,' says Nick Hoggett of DPA Lighting Consultants. 'You still see so much fluorescent or cold cathode and they're not right for fine dining or even a brasserie. The xenon lamp is basically a tungsten festoon filled with xenon gas, to give it a 10,000 hour life – so you get the softness and dimmability of tungsten with the long life of a discharge lamp. It's a great source for restaurants.'

Mary Rushton-Beales of Lighting Design House believes it is perhaps too easy to overlight covings and cornices and that the original object can therefore be defeated. 'You do have to be careful with cove lighting because you end up almost always with more lighting than you need and it has to be dimmed. Also if you're not careful you end up with more even light when you want a bit more drama and mood.'

Time, Newcastle, UK by Paul Daly – directional rather than diffuse downlighting is more effective in creating atmosphere (overleaf). PHOTOGRAPH BY ADRIAN WILSON.

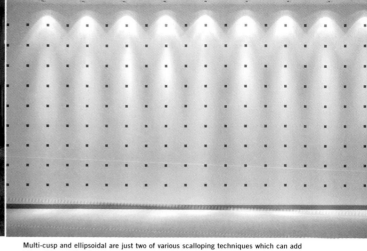

Light giving and decorative element: wall fittings at Floriana, London, UK by Lighting Design International. PHOTOGRAPH COURTESY OF LIGHTING DESIGN INTERNATIONAL.

At Tavern on the Green in Crawley, UK by Marlin Lighting, lighting effects on the far wall are used to create warmth and visual stimulation in what could be an intimidating space. PHOTOGRAPH COURTESY OF MARLIN LIGHTING.

Multi-cusp and ellipsoidal are just two of various scalloping techniques which can add interest to a wall surface. PHOTOGRAPHS © ZUMTOBEL LIGHTING.

Wall lighting

The lighting of vertical surfaces is important because that is where the eye naturally falls – we rarely scrutinise the floor or the ceiling.

A wall-mounted up/downlighter is one of the most basic ways of achieving quite stunning effects – according to the nature of the diffuser, the source used and the control of light output and direction they can vary from soft wash to more dramatic patterning. They are also a decorative opportunity – with styles ranging from candle sconces to Scandinavian minimalism, all aesthetics are covered – and they can be exploited for logos and motifs.

Walls can be softly washed from above – from ceiling recessed low voltage downlights, or from track-mounted compact fluorescent fittings, though fluorescent might well be too cool for a bar/restaurant environment. Coloured light projections or washes can be used as a decorative element, particularly effective in countering the coldness of a large space, while low level wall-mounted uplighting makes a dramatic statement, reminiscent of footlights. Walls will also be lit incidentally if artworks, sculptures and other wall-mounted decorative elements are being highlighted.

Scalloping – achieved usually with a line of low voltage downlights or fibre optic light heads to create a series of decorative scoops along a wall – has become one of those ubiquitous and possibly overrated wall lighting techniques, which when done well can be striking, but when done badly looks like a dog's dinner. A common mistake is to use a cluttered rather than clean vertical surface with everything from the tops of doorways to ventilation outlets disrupting and confusing the flow of the pattern. (This is an area where the early collaboration of lighting designer, interior designer and architect can help so that the position of wallwashers and other regular arrays can be co-ordinated.) Scalloping can sometimes result by accident,

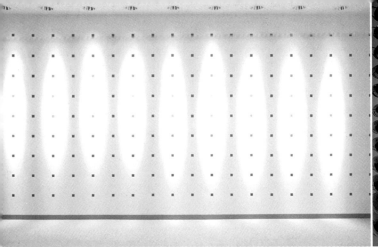

Philippe Starck's backlighting of bottles at Teatriz, Madrid, Spain demonstrates the potential of light and glass for optics or back-of-bar displays.

The slim circular T5 fluorescent lamp from Philips Lighting, is used to backlight the bar at Che café/bar, London, UK.
PHOTOGRAPH COURTESY OF PHILIPS LIGHTING.

though rarely a happy one, when wallwashers designed for a more uniform effect have been positioned too close to the wall. Another problem is that insufficient attention is often paid to lining up and balancing the pattern in the first place, or it becomes disturbed through less than careful maintenance. One solution is to use a fitting with its own reflector so that the beam width can't be altered when the fitting is relamped by someone not *au fait* with, or unconcerned by, the original spec.

The function of focal points

Creating contrasts in particular spaces serves a functional, as well as decorative purpose. The human eye is automatically drawn to brightly lit elements or areas. Illumination can therefore serve to orientate or attract people. The cash desk or the bar, for instance, are likely to be more brightly lit than the surrounding space in order to attract attention and, in the latter case, to provide a focal point.

Where bars are concerned, the major considerations are that the staff behind it look good, that the view behind them looks attractive and that they are able to see well enough to perform their tasks.

Optics can be backlit – light and glass are a perfect marriage – but precautions need to be taken against glare to staff and customers, possibly through the use of dimmers.

As one of the key horizontal surfaces, the top of the bar is a prime area for downlighting (it is a functional area, staff have to see what they are doing), either with surface-mounted low voltage tungsten halogen spots, recessed fittings, fittings concealed in the glasses rack above the bar or often with decorative pendants, again usually with the crisp, white light of halogen. Aside from the advantages of their light quality, halogen lamps with cool beam reflectors give off very little heat in the direction of the beam (the dichroic coating on the reflector directs the infrared backwards so around 60 per cent of

the heat is dissipated behind the lamp), which is useful if warm beer is to be avoided or there is bar-top food.

Increasingly the bar is becoming an architectural element to exploit and the lighting of it has become commensurately more adventurous. It is an area where cheaper and cheerful sources such as fluorescent – used with coloured gels to backlight glass frontages – can come into their own, and where fibre optics or cold cathode – trimming the base and top of the bar, for instance – can produce sophisticated and often spectacular effects. The bar top itself can also be backlit (ideal with materials such as onyx, alabaster, etched glass or resin) for an ethereal glow – very Star Trek.

Ambient lighting

The sum total of light used to model the space will usually be sufficient to provide the requisite ambient lighting, unless the space is particularly barn-like or the intention is to have high light levels because it is appropriate to the image of the venue. (The control system, see page 28, can allow for sufficient light levels for functional purposes such as cleaning).

'I would aim 90 per cent of the time not to have ambient lighting as such,' says Mary Rushton-Beales. 'You highlight the architectural features, you light the tables, you light whatever features there are in the space and that is usually enough to give you sufficient ambient lighting. The only places where you get higher ambient levels are in more minimalist interiors where you are aiming for a very clean, ever so bright effect.'

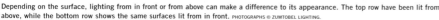

Depending on the surface, lighting from in front or from above can make a difference to its appearance. The top row have been lit from above, while the bottom row shows the same surfaces lit from in front. PHOTOGRAPHS © ZUMTOBEL LIGHTING.

A combination of linear fluorescent with colour gels and low voltage dichroic exploit the varying textures of steel, soft linen and shattered glass at the Chelsea Brasserie, London, UK by Marlin Lighting. PHOTOGRAPH COURTESY OF MARLIN LIGHTING.

Surfaces

Light in itself is invisible. It only becomes visible when it strikes an object or a surface. The subtlety of that interaction is, however, enormous. In his book *Planning and Designing Lighting*, US lighting designer Edward Effron encapsulated our ability to distinguish between objects and elements using light:

'Reflection allows you to differentiate between a puddle and a wet street. You can tell the fine fishbone from the white flesh of a fish because the two reflect light differently.'

Colour and the nature of materials therefore have a huge influence on the impact of lighting. The reflective qualities of different substances vary enormously, either swallowing the light completely like black tweed, or like stainless steel, bouncing it straight off in different directions.

While white reflects 70–80 per cent of the light which reaches it, black only reflects four per cent. Maple and birch have a reflectivity of 60 per cent, red brick 5–25 per cent, concrete 15–40 per cent and glass 6–8 per cent. The colour and materials used in an interior will accordingly make a difference to lighting strategy. The impact of those colours and materials can also, in turn, be orchestrated by the type of lighting.

'It's always fun to play with different textures and surfaces and to play them off one against another, either accentuating them or playing them down with light – with a different colour filter, for example,' says Mary Rushton-Beales. 'Or you can use the colour temperature of the light – you might use mains voltage halogen to make certain materials warmer and low voltage tungsten halogen where you want a crisper effect.'

Sources

Lighting in a restaurant or bar should in particular flatter flesh tones and the food, which is why the selection of light source is crucial. In the supermarket, for instance, metal halide – at the cool end of the lighting spectrum – freshens the fish counter, while white son or tungsten halogen 'warm' the meat or the fruit section, playing to the colours at the red end of the spectrum. Food and flesh tones in the bar or restaurant need to be considered in the same way. Most international standards recommend that lamps conform at least to colour rendering categories 1B and 2A (70Ra–90Ra).

Sources such as white son or the more recent ceramic metal halide (designed to counter the colour shift problems of quartz metal halide) perhaps have potential in the future, while CDM is a comparatively 'warm' source, it may still be too cool for most upmarket bar/restaurant environments. In addition, the difficulty with dimming these discharge lamps is an enormous barrier.

For that reason, where primary sources are concerned, tungsten halogen, both mains voltage and low voltage, remains the most commonly specified lamp type. The crisp, white light of low voltage dichroics is complimentary to cutlery and glassware, its beam control makes it ideal for highlighting decorative elements such as artworks or flowers, and dimmed it becomes increasingly similar to candlelight, warm and flattering to skin tones.

However, there is a danger of a distinct similarity between restaurants of a certain type, to say nothing of a universal blandness. 'The variation comes by adding, say, subtle gels for colour or by using a combination of mains voltage and low voltage,' suggests Mary Rushton-Beales. 'I've mixed par 20s and par 30s with low voltage tungsten halogen and there is a difference in colour temperature – you can sharpen that distinction particularly if, for instance, you use the warmer light on a warmer surface. You get a more interesting picture that way.'

Fibre optics – colour changing on the back wall, scalloping the bar front and (not shown) buried into the wall throwing light across the walkway – transform the bar at Babe Ruth's, London, UK by Marlin Lighting into a dynamic decorative feature (facing). PHOTOGRAPH COURTESY OF MARLIN LIGHTING.

The classic fibre optic starry sky treatment in the Members Club Room, Cliveden, Berkshire, UK. PHOTOGRAPH COURTESY OF ABSOLUTE ACTION.

Fibre optics dramatise the perspective at the Voodoo Lounge in London, UK. PHOTOGRAPH COURTESY OF PHILIPS LIGHTING.

The Base Bar, London, UK by Baynes and Co., where the entire lighting scheme relies on fibre optics. PHOTOGRAPH BY VIEWPOINT.

Special effects

Fibre optics

Other lighting elements within the space are also an antidote to insipidity. Because of its decorative and dynamic lighting possibilities – especially colour changing – fibre optics is ideal for the restaurant and bar environment and there are signs of its increasing use in this area.

Unfortunately, it has been dogged to some extent by a reputation for being costly and for not delivering on promise, largely as a result of cowboy companies rather than any intrinsic problem with the technology. In fact that technology has improved greatly over the last decade – more powerful lamps, more sophisticated lenses have led to an increase in the length of the tails (generally about ten to 15 metres before there is deterioration in the quality of light) and an improved viability for more general solutions.

Decorative possibilities range from the classic starry sky ceiling to subtle pinpoints of light over a bar area, to scalloping of the bar front. Side-emitting fibre optics can offer even funkier and more flamboyant applications.

Because technological developments have led to an increase in light output, there is more than one instance of fibre optics being the sole light source in a bar/restaurant environment. Maintenance is obviously one issue here, especially if lighting needs to be positioned in an awkward or relatively inaccessible location, and was the driving force behind their installation in the Fleetwood public house and wine bar in London. Rather than having to relamp at all 200 light points only 12 lamps need to be changed in the remotely positioned light boxes or engines. The versatility of fibre optics is also clearly demonstrated with different lenses creating scalloping effects, downlighting and accent lighting.

00 colour change projectors from wash the walls of Yo! Sushi, London, PHOTOGRAPH COURTESY OF ETC.

A gobo is used to project the name of 36 restaurant in Edinburgh, Scotland. PHOTOGRAPH COURTESY OF JONATHAN SPEIRS AND ASSOCIATES.

Projected hieroglyphics pick up the Egyptian motif at the Pyramid Club, Dubai by Lighting Design House. PHOTOGRAPH BY GERRY RUSHTON-BEALES.

Paul Daly uses cold cathode to simply outline the bar at Time, Newcastle, UK. PHOTOGRAPH BY ADRIAN WILSON.

Gobos/projectors

Architectural lighting in general has gradually become permeated with theatrical lighting techniques and modified theatrical equipment. Where only a few years ago colour changing projectors might have been dismissed as a tad vulgar, coloured light generally has now become more acceptable, and so has the idea of dynamic light. There is clearly huge potential for these techniques in restaurant and bar environments. Where certain areas of the market are concerned, the experience of eating out has in itself become more of a theatrical event, the Planet Hollywood chain being the most obvious and literal example. But the implication is not necessarily rock 'n' roll. Colour change can be slow and subtle and, used judiciously, as appropriate to the more dignified end of the dining spectrum as the trendy bar.

Gobos – painted, etched or cut out images placed in front of a narrow beam luminaire so the image is projected on to a distant surface – have also long moved from simply suggesting woodlands or church windows on the theatrical stage to more commercial applications. The images can be static or moving.

As a decorative element, they are a simple but effective way of dealing with a yawning space, perhaps creating dappled light across a large expanse of floor, or texturing a blank wall. From the simple projection of a restaurant logo on the pavement outside, to enhancing foliage with moving leaf patterns, to the recreation of the passage of the sun from rising to setting in a bar space, the possibilities are infinite.

Cold cathode

Neon has a time-honoured association with the bar/restaurant milieu in the form of signage, while the related but more practical (and brighter) cold cathode technology can be used for a variety of purposes in interiors. Easily dimmed, low voltage and with a long life, it can be used as an overt decorative element to frame bars or optic areas, for instance, or as a concealed source – in coving, behind banquettes, integrated into the base of bench seating – to lend warm white light or soft glowing colours to ceilings, walls and floors.

Side-emitting fibre optics produce a flamboyant finish at Caesar's Palace, Liverpool, UK (overleaf). PHOTOGRAPH COURTESY OF GRADUS LIGHTING.

Luminaire as centrepiece: reproduction lanterns at the Hopetoun Restaurant, West Lothian, Scotland. COURTESY OF KEVAN SHAW LIGHTING DESIGN. PHOTOGRAPH BY TAPIO ROSENIUS.

Luminaire in fancy dress: Le Bar Bat, New York, USA. COURTESY OF FOCUS LIGHTING. PHOTOGRAPH BY PAUL WARCHOL.

Low voltage downlighting is used in the deeper set part of Bobby's Bar, Portugal to balance the daylight at the front. PHOTOGRAPH COURTESY OF UNITED DESIGNERS.

Fitting to be seen

To return to the introduction, it is significant that Patrick Caulfield is preoccupied with the phenomenon of light itself, and rather less with the luminaire that is emitting it. Despite the fact that correct lighting levels can kill or cure a restaurant space, too often the interior designer homes in on the aesthetics of the fitting at the expense of the light effect it produces.

Whatever the environment, lighting design at its purest makes the fitting as discreet as possible – the effect is all. One lighting designer once expressed a preference for a particular Italian luminaire for restaurants, a wall up/downlighter, because it disappeared when illuminated. 'It's the light pattern you see, not the fitting,' he enthused.

However, unless the approach is to aim entirely for lighting effect – recessed ceiling fittings, concealed lighting in ceiling covings or behind seating – the aesthetics of the fitting are clearly part of the interior motif, and often a centrepiece. The chandelier has been associated with fine dining since time immemorial and it is hardly a byword for discretion.

It is an area which Sally Storey sees as one of mutual co-operation between the interior and lighting designer. 'The fitting is a decorative item that is to be selected by the interior designer. Our job is to make it work for that scheme. I think we can do quite a lot by adapting the light source. If they found a fitting they liked that had a compact fluorescent lamp and I didn't think that was appropriate, I would see if it could be adapted to a tungsten. Or if they had a fitting which gave a particularly sharp light effect I'd look at controlling it individually. So you'd still get the look of the fitting but it would be softened, perhaps by dimming. Or I could look at the colour of the shade. One needs to be involved but you don't have to select the fittings.'

And in the often heavily themed environment of the bar/restaurant, there is frequently fun to be had with the fitting. Focus Lighting's scheme for Le Bar Bat in New York, where the luminaire has been turned into a flying bat, proves the point.

Daylight and glazing

The two main factors which decide people whether or not to enter a restaurant on spec are the menu (which therefore needs to be well illuminated at night) and how appealing the place appears inside. Most restaurants and many bars therefore have a high degree of glazing on the shop window principle.

As some examples later in this book demonstrate, daylighting brings its own atmosphere and can have a stunning effect on the interior. But depending on the volume of natural light flooding in, it can give rise to a number of issues. First, it can militate against an intimate atmosphere if that is the nature of the venue.

Second, depending on the location and orientation of the site, there is a potential problem of glare and too much heat from sunlight. This can be resolved with the obvious methods of diffusion, the curtain or the blind – which can exploit the qualities of natural light rather than just blocking it – or by the glass itself.

Whatever the season, low light transmission glass does tend to render the scene outside perennially winter, however, while fritted glass can have the effect of a lace curtain when viewed from the outside in, so it needs careful application. But the latter, produced by screen printing images in ceramic paint or ink, then firing the glass, does have the benefit of acting as a medium for drawings, patterns or logos.

The third area to be addressed is the likely imbalance of light between the area nearest the glazing and the deeper set space, which needs to be compensated for with higher ambient light. Sally Storey suggests a range of techniques to solve variations in illumination levels.

'That's when you need lighting controls for one thing. You can use low voltage – the daylight can sometimes become the ambient lighting and the low voltage the sparkle in between. Or you could even have panels backlit with fluorescent, as long as the colour temperature is right and it doesn't look like an office.

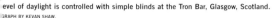
evel of daylight is controlled with simple blinds at the Tron Bar, Glasgow, Scotland. GRAPH BY KEVAN SHAW.

An artificial skylight in Sir Terence Conran's Quaglino's, London, UK lightens a basement location. PHOTOGRAPH COURTESY OF MARLIN LIGHTING.

At Floriana in London, Lighting Design International tricks the eye by gradually reducing light levels on the stairs to the basement. PHOTOGRAPH COURTESY OF LIGHTING DESIGN INTERNATIONAL.

Faking daylight

Often what's also effective if you've got strong daylight in one area is to give a wallwash effect to the other wall, so you feel that it's not a dark wall at the other end.'

The fourth issue is the effect at night if some form of diffusion is not used on the glazing – which it won't be if there is a half way decent view, for instance. In that case, the main object will be to cause as little interference with the view as possible, either from too high light levels obliterating the scene or through too much reflection from badly positioned or directed fittings. Dimmed down levels and shielded luminaires mounted at the side of the windows, for instance, will both help avoid the problem.

Ideally, if there is any kind of landscape outside the window, even if it's only a terrace, lighting of trees or just the simple pinspotting of a sculpture or attractive plant will not only look exotic, but will also help the eye through the glazing and past any residual distracting reflections.

Not all restaurants or bars are at ground level, of course. Those in a basement location, or any situation where there is no glazing, have to avoid the problem of Stygian gloom – an effect which can be apparent as much as actual if during daylight hours there is too much contrast between the natural light outside and the artificial light which greets patrons as they enter. One solution is the fake skylight which can be highly effective in recreating natural exterior light patterns. This is largely achieved by backlighting with fluorescent sources of different colour temperatures combined with cold cathode – dimming and mixing between the lamps creates lighting effects which correspond to changing light levels outside.

'I like this technique because you can control it,' says Miles Pinniger. 'You can change its intensity and its colour during the day and at night you can make it turn dark blue. It's usually quite a low budget job too.'

Otherwise, if the ceiling is not too low, lighting it – perhaps from recessed uplights in the floor to cast pools of light or through concealed lighting in cornices – will help to give a feeling of volume and counter the effect of a dark plane overhead. Projecting images or patterns takes the technique a step further. Where the ceiling is lower, lighting the walls will make the space appear lighter because the eye goes naturally to a vertical surface and there will also be a degree of reflected light in the space. Sally Storey maintains that the daytime scene is the main one to consider because of the marked variation in light levels, and that in a basement location, for instance, the solution is to play on the eye's capacity to adapt to different lighting conditions.

'In the evening it's less of a problem because you're not competing with daylight. What you want is to try and make the entrance, which is usually at ground level, quite bright initially and then guide people down by reducing the light levels down the stairs – that can be done quite dramatically. You can light each tread individually, for example, which is fun. This reduction in light level will make the iris retract. Then you can make the space downstairs slightly brighter, so when you come into the restaurant it seems bright and airy again.'

Tridonic's digital dimming system demonstrates some of the different scenes that can be created with lighting controls.

Lighting control systems

The importance of a control system in a bar or restaurant cannot be overemphasised. It is the ultimate tool for creating and fine tuning the desired ambience and atmosphere. The ambient lighting that is appropriate to a lunch-time scene with full daylight outside is an entirely different story from late evening when it is dark and people are more relaxed.

They can also allow a degree of commercial manipulation. The fact that brighter conditions deter people from lingering has been established earlier. The implication is that restaurants are in two camps – the fast turnover venues with higher light levels and those with more subtle light patterns for relaxed and presumably better quality dining. But the control system also allows a single restaurant to combine both those scenarios to a degree.

At lunch-time a restaurant may well be catering to a quick turnover crowd taking an hour out of the working day. (Although this applies less to Mediterranean countries where the lunch-time meal is invested with more importance). Those brighter conditions can be toned down and mellowed for the evening session when patrons can afford more time and can be encouraged to stay longer and spend more money.

From a highly practical viewpoint, the predominant source in most bars and restaurants is low voltage tungsten halogen, the lamp life of which can be doubled when connected to dimmers. Quality dimmers can extend that to five times normal life.

If a control system is installed, there should not be a single front-of-house source that cannot be dimmed. 'One of the key factors in restaurant and bar design is that every bit of lighting should be dimmable,' says Mary Rushton-Beales. 'If it's not, that one element will glare at you at late night level.'

And, as Sally Storey points out, it is crucial to ensure that the system is installed correctly. 'There may be a control system with presets, but all too often they're zoned in areas, rather than for effect, because installation has been left to the contractors.

So real opportunities are missed – for example, in large restaurants you have the noise and the bustle, but at the same time you could use the lighting to sub-divide and break up the space.'

Some venues have complex and highly sophisticated scene setting – one British restaurant/pub chain has 64 different light scenes over a seven-day period. If this is all on a pre-set system and there is no need for manual override, then complexity is less of a problem. But if the system is to be operated by the *mâitre d'*, for instance, as it is in a lot of cases, then a simplified system is sometimes not only adequate but a positive advantage.

'It needs to be relatively simple,' says Sally Storey. 'You need lunch, which could double up as a cleaning setting, early evening and late evening. It's harder for people to operate with any more. Manual override is important because of the way the moods change or you have different crowds in – you may not change to the late evening setting because it's an older crowd in that night, for example.'

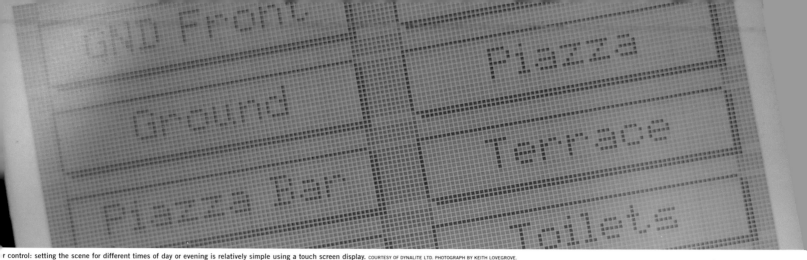

r control: setting the scene for different times of day or evening is relatively simple using a touch screen display. COURTESY OF DYNALITE LTD. PHOTOGRAPH BY KEITH LOVEGROVE.

Lighting control systems checklist: what to consider

1. Before selecting a system, establish the functionality of the restaurant and its target market. If it is part of a chain, it is crucial that systems are identical in all venues – for corporate identity and to enable staff to move between sites with minimal retraining.

2. Consider the atmosphere that should be created at different times of the day so that the sophistication of the control system needed can be established.

3. Transitions between scenes should be smooth and almost imperceptible.

4. While the wall box dimmer offers the cheapest dimming available, they have several shortcomings – it is not possible to accurately repeat a setting; it is difficult to subtly change the lighting while diners are in the restaurant; they are not renowned for long term reliability; they are prone to flicker.

5. Position the control panel where the restaurant space can be clearly seen, but not where the public has access to it. There should also be a panel at the staff entrance/exit door with a simple on/off control, ideally with a key-locking switch on it.

6. Manual override is an important facility – for raising the light levels for speeches at a wedding, for dimming the light right down for the arrival of a birthday cake...

7. Make sure the system can be extended or modified simply and cheaply.

8. Make sure maintained emergency light fittings only turn to full-on when there is a power failure or a circuit breaker trips – not when the system reaches the late dinner scene.

(Source: David Kerr, Dynalite, manufacturers of architectural dimmers and building control systems.)

en sink drama: at the Tour de France restaurant at the Pyramid Club in Dubai (LIGHTING DESIGN HOUSE, PHOTOGRAPH BY GERRY RUSHTON-BEALES) (above) and Babe Ruth's, London, UK (PHOTOGRAPH COURTESY OF MARLIN LIGHTING) (above right), the kitchen moves
front of house and lighting treatment changes accordingly.

Less considered areas

WCs

In the past it has often been too easy to pay all the attention to front of house and literally go for the bog standard approach in the washrooms. It has probably been as much to do with priorities and attention to detail as budget. But as patrons are becoming generally more demanding and have higher expectations, it is increasingly an area that is being addressed and which is improving.

Harsh (usually over cool fluorescent) and badly positioned lighting has resulted over the years in the application of tons of superfluous blusher as women have attempted to counter the Bella Lugosi effect. Even in more upmarket environs, there is often a tendency to get it wrong, particularly where the ladies room is concerned.

'The typical designer mistake is to highlight the sink,' says Dominic Meyrick. 'Don't do that because effectively as a female you're going to be ducking in and out of this very dynamic light pattern. Always set the light fittings away from the mirror – come into the left and right of somebody as they're walking towards the mirror, bearing in mind that the sink dictates where the person goes. And don't get the source pointing at the mirror because the reflection will cause glare.'

Sally Storey is an advocate of the control system in WCs. 'The lighting needs to be a bit brighter than elsewhere so that you can see your face but basically the levels should change with those of the restaurant – because what's the point of being in a moody restaurant then going into brightly lit loos?'

And a word of advice when it comes to the gents. 'Don't highlight a urinal,' adds Meyrick. 'Men don't need to know where to pee and if the urinal is not kept clean then it looks appalling.' Unless, of course, it's a design classic, like a Philippe Starck urinal.

Kitchens

Kitchens should not only be well lit to allow staff to feel comfortable and be able to perform their tasks efficiently (there are regulations governing this), but there is an increasing fashion for them to be on view to patrons. Aesthetic as well as practical considerations must therefore come into play. Somehow the transition between the functional fluorescent invariably used for the kitchen and the intimacy of tungsten halogen inevitably used for the restaurant space must be smoothed. 'I've just used shower-proof recessed tungsten halogen downlights because you have to do something that can be cleaned,' says Mary Rushton-Beales. 'And you really must try not to put fluorescent where it shows.'

'If the kitchen is part of the conversation then it should be lit in a new and dynamic way,' says Dominic Meyrick. 'It's part of the atmosphere of the space. Of course it has to conform to all the necessary standards, and provide certain light levels so that tasks can be carried out, but that doesn't mean it has to be dull.'

When kitchens are not on display, it is easy to overlook that back and front of house are nevertheless linked and that the former can impact on the latter. 'We look at the door swings and the way the lobbies are arranged so that we reduce the glare from the fluorescent which often kills the scheme in the restaurant itself. If they have glazing in the swing door we might look at putting a filter over that,' says Sally Storey.

Slash with a dash: the Catwalk Café, Edinburgh, Scotland by Stoane Associated Architects and Mike Stoane Lighting (facing). PHOTOGRAPH BY LESLEY JONES.

Supermarket coffee shops such as Sainsbury's J's (PHOTOGRAPH COURTESY OF PINNIGER AND PARTNERS) (above left) and large outlets like Babe Ruth's (PHOTOGRAPH COURTESY OF MARLIN LIGHTING) (above centre and right) are more likely to feature discharge lighting because of context and scale respectively.

Specialist venues: breaking the rules

Supermarket coffee shops

As shopping becomes increasingly a leisure pursuit rather than a necessity, and as supermarkets battle ruthlessly for market share using added-value services as part of their armoury, the growth in the number of coffee shops in supermarket locations has become marked. And so has the improvement in quality among existing outlets.

Because of the nature of their context, many lighting precepts that apply to other eateries have to be modified if not reversed. 'This is definitely an area where you could use cold cathode or fluorescent and it works well,' says Miles Pinniger, who has created the lighting schemes for Sainsbury's J's coffee shops. 'Xenon might work well in a bistro environment but here you want something brisker.'

The primary reason – apart from the fact that supermarkets don't want customers hanging around there all day – is that the coffee shop is invariably adjacent to the retail area, a space which has notoriously high light levels.

'Usually the customer is coming out of the supermarket lit to thousands of lux and if you light the restaurant area to traditional levels the brightness contrast is just too severe – they look so gloomy when viewed from the store,' says Pinniger.

However, the overall result is a matter of mixing sources – low voltage tungsten halogen will still commonly be used over the food servery, for instance – achieving the compromise between seguing contrasting light levels and creating a welcoming space that will tempt customers to take a break from shopping.

The mega restaurant

Another type of venue that is an exception to the tungsten halogen rule is the large, multi-purpose, often family-orientated outlet. At London's Babe Ruth's, which in addition to bar and video games area, has a general 300-seater feature restaurant and a second 100-seater back restaurant, the wall heights are more than four metres. The scale of the space is such that with the exception of some low voltage lighting on a canopy to give a scalloping effect to one wall, lighting designer Dominic Meyrick relied totally on discharge sources.

Ambient lighting is supplied by twin 32W compact fluorescent downlighters capable of dimming. 'Although it's a big cavern of a space it's also got to get moody at some stage which means we had to be able to drop the light level,' says Meyrick. Columns are picked out with ceramic metal halide, as is the mural, using pull out and direct fittings.

Decorative 'clouds' suspended from the ceiling have fluorescent tubes, one with a blue sleeve, the other with a red which through mixing and dimming create a colour change effect from one to the other through all shades of purple.

'Fluorescent is reinventing itself,' says Meyrick. 'Somewhere along the way these types of sources can become useful, especially as we get more into this idea of the eating machine, the big restaurant with the 400–500 seater scenario.'

lights: contrasting impressions of Bobby Jones Bar, Portugal (PHOTOGRAPH COURTESY OF UNITED DESIGNERS) (above); Expo Café, Hanover, Germany (PHOTOGRAPH COURTESY OF ULRIKE BRANDI LICHT) (above right).

Cultural differences

While there are some universal precepts about good lighting, there are nevertheless exceptions depending on the part of the world under discussion. Perceptions can be coloured by culture or by climate. While in northern climes, for instance, fluorescent lighting at the cooler end of the Ra scale is frequently regarded as too harsh a source in certain environments, it is the preferred lamp in warmer zones such as southern Europe or tropical and sub-tropical Asia. In Japan it is the most common source in domestic environments.

This globalization of attitudes should not be overemphasised but it can occasionally lead to conflicting messages for the lighting designer.

'Cultural preferences are significant,' says lighting designer Michael Huggins of Hong Kong-based Light Directions. 'Chinese restaurants are a case in point. I have learnt that whatever a Chinese client may say beforehand, they actually want their restaurants bright – even when they are trying to achieve a Western feel. Often you return to a Chinese restaurant a few weeks after commissioning and setting comfortable and dramatic evening dimming settings on the lighting control system, only to find the restaurant operating in housekeeping or full-on mode.'

Exterior impressions

Exactly as a shop window is designed to attract potential customers into the store, so the exterior of a bar or restaurant advertises its presence, its image, the nature of its cuisine, the prices it charges. An outlet in an isolated position will obviously need to make its presence felt if it is either to be located easily or attract passing custom. By the same token so will a restaurant in a busy high street where it has to compete for attention.

Many restaurants and bars are goldfish bowls. Exterior lighting is likely to be limited to illumination of the name, the menu and, though too often neglected, the entrance. In the evening, it is most often the role of the lighting inside that is coming into play and potentially creating a huge impact outside. That role is simple, but fundamental.

'The obvious thing that we all take for granted is that the lighting is what tells you whether the restaurant is inviting or indeed open for business,' says Miles Pinniger. 'It's the key cue – if you're wandering around a strange town looking for somewhere to eat, then the lighting is what will decide you at least to move in the direction of that place to look at it.'

Like moths with flames, human beings find light irresistible.

proje

section two

The gentle early morning sunshine which mellows breakfast at a pavement café. The soft, smoky haze of a mid-afternoon bar. The clean, brittle light of an all-night diner. Light is capable of expressing an enormous range of moods. From the minimalist interplay of light and shadow in a Japanese restaurant to the star-spangled manner of the American theme venue, the following case studies illustrate how richly diverse the approach to lighting can be – and how it can be woven into the very fabric of a bar or restaurant's identity.

Satsuma, London, UK
Architects/lighting: Stiff + Trevillion

PHOTOGRAPH © MORLEY VON STERNBERG

'As an all-day restaurant, both daylight and artificial light need to work in harmony.'

Satsuma is an essay in the Japanese principles of light and shade. A fast-turnover Japanese food restaurant at the budget end of the scale, it has two thirds of the dining area in the basement and the remainder at ground-floor level. Daylight is a key component in the overall scheme – and much play is made of shadow. The orientation of the building benefits from natural light and it has been introduced to both levels of the restaurant by creating vertical volumes around the staircase and shopfront, allowing light to

Creating vertical volumes around the staircase and shop-front allows light to penetrate into the basement (facing).

'The volumes, textures and colours
were carefully selected

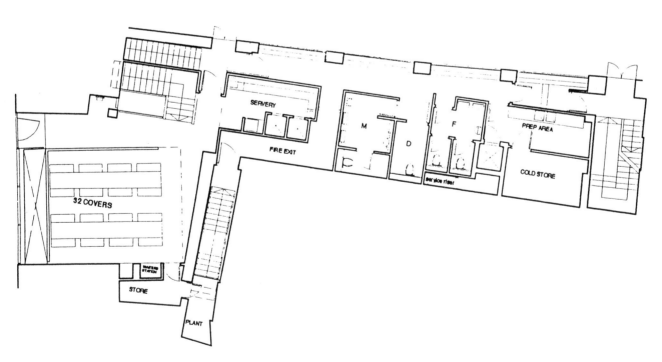

penetrate into the basement. Artificial light, supplied by Illuma Lighting and Basis Design, was used as a further means of layering the spaces. 'As an all-day restaurant, both daylight and artificial light need to work in harmony,' says Richard Blandy of Stiff + Trevillion. 'The volumes, textures and colours were carefully selected to emphasise shadow as well as light.' In the upper restaurant a white blind is used to control the sunlight which streams through the west facing window. Internally it is a feature in its own right as shadows and light change through the afternoon. At night, backlit, it becomes a large illuminated sign for the restaurant.

o emphasise shadow as well as light.'

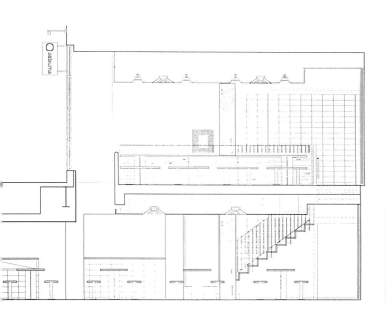

Lights of passage: in the washroom corridor blocks of colour lit with low energy lamps become sources in themselves (above).

Artificial lighting – dimmed low voltage – highlights the tables. Downstairs, directional low voltage fittings are also used for the tables and for simple scalloping effects on the perimeter walls. The kitchen has a semi-industrial fluorescent glow indicating the function of the space. Natural materials with a limited palette – rough timber, solid ash, shuttered concrete, smooth plaster – have been used throughout with constant consideration given to their interplay with simple lighting effects. The circulation route to the WCs, for instance, is lit with low-level PLC lamps to create a series of coloured reflections on the white blinds.

'The washroom corridor and escape route use bold Corbusian colour to create a passage of light and colour,' says Blandy. 'The pigment becomes a reflective light source – the strong blocks of colour applied to the plaster walls become light sources in themselves.'

One Happy Cloud, Stockholm, Sweden
Architects/designer/lighting: Claesson Koivisto Rune Arkitektkontor

'At night we wanted to key the light to the atmosphere, according to how many people there were. During the daytime, the daylight floats into the space.'

The aim of One Happy Cloud was not to be yet another sushi bar. The menu is about simple cooking but unusually blends Japanese and Swedish cuisines. That amalgam is also present in the lighting and design philosophy. It reflects the tradition of both cultures for light, uncomplicated interiors and a sense of spatial calm. Designed along two intersecting axes, one axis of the restaurant runs parallel with the street allowing a high degree of natural daylight into the space, providing the primary source of light apart from fluorescent lighting by Finnish company Ensto Hovik. This suspended system boldly slices through the space from one end of the restaurant to the other, some 16 metres, spearing walls and even the blackboard artwork.

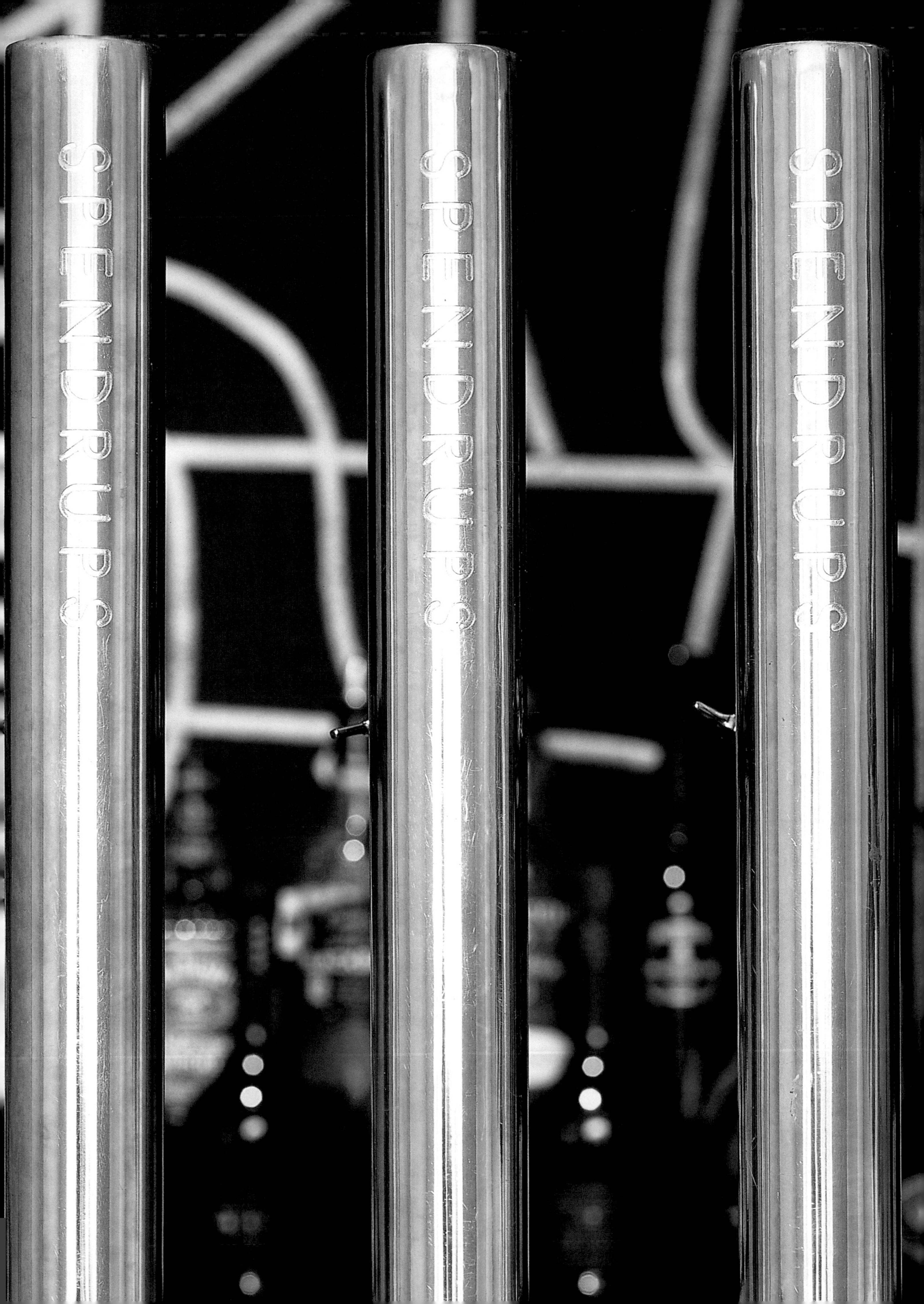
SPENDRUPS
SPENDRUPS
SPENDRUPS

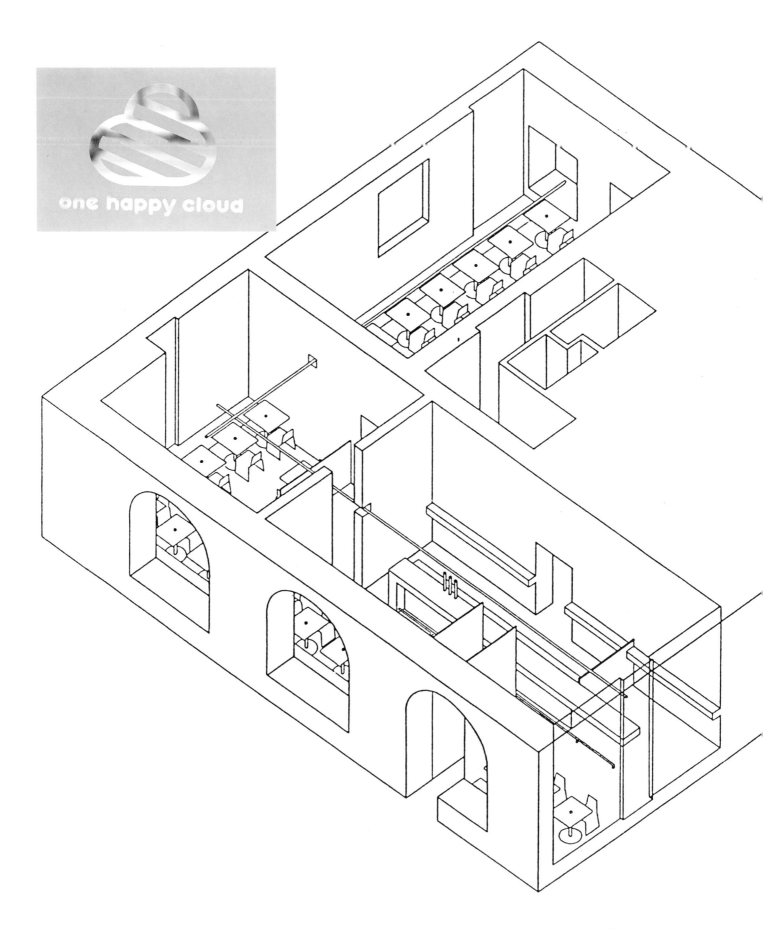

one happy cloud

In Sweden where daylight hours are extended, the preference is for minimal artificial light. At night, the fluorescent system is dimmed almost to orange and the space is lit by candles. In a contemporary twist on a classic restaurant tradition, glass candle holders by Finnish company Marimekko are sunk into the specially designed tables to become a design detail. 'At night we wanted to key the light to the atmosphere, according to how many people there were,' says architect Ola Rune. 'During the daytime, the daylight floats into the space.'

Veeraswamy, London, UK
Lighting designer: Lighting Design International. Designer: Bilkey Llinas

PHOTOGRAPH © NICHOLAS KANE facing and overleaf

'The very strong colours on the walls needed light to really bring out the drama.'

Veeraswamy is not only London's oldest Indian restaurant but one of its most fashionable. The aim of a recent refurbishment was to retain a sense of traditional opulence with gold finishes and rich colours, but to spice them with a fresh and contemporary approach. The lighting, the budget for which was a modest £11,000, was intended as a primary design feature and Lighting Design International worked closely with interior designers Bilkey Llinas to complement the effects they were trying to achieve. The main difficulty, says Sally Storey of LDI, was 'to maintain continuity across four very different areas while still keeping an element of individuality'.

Dividing the main body of the restaurant is a glass partition. The translucency of the glass was exploited with uplighting from Reggiani 50mm spots so that the lower half of the screen glimmers with a bluish light. The same fittings were also used to uplight the half columns on the walls to create a glow from within and to backlight the gold leaf patterns. The most overt form of lighting is from traditional freestanding lamps with Belgian linen shades which illuminate the tables. The reflective qualities of glass are again used to effectively with the bottle display which occupies a dominant position in the main area of the restaurant. Genesis Magnifix downlights (chosen for ease of relamping) make the glass sparkle and the gold background gleam.

Elsewhere uplighting is used to simple but stunning effect to graze the curved gold wall in a separate section of the restaurant. Whereas a typical technique would be to recess the fittings in the floor, here the Modular Argus wall-mounted uplights create a decorative element in themselves as a horizontal row of 'studs'.

On peripheral walls and framing the window arches are Delta up/downlights, painted to wall finish and coloured by dichroic filters to complement the colour of the room. At one end, decorative locks mounted on glass panels are picked out with Concord Myriad recessed adjustable low voltage downlights. Small and discreet, the fitting has a parabolic reflector and pull-out head which helped get a tighter angle of focus on the locks. 'The very strong colours on the walls needed light to really bring out the drama,' says Ranjit Mahani, chairman of Chelsea Plaza Restaurants which owns Veeraswamy. 'The challenge was using the lighting in a manner which produced variety without appearing bitty and without being extravagant in terms of cost.'

The reflective qualities of glass are fully exploited with uplighting of the glass room divider (left) and tight spotlighting of the wine display (above).

Browns Café Bar, Coventry, UK
Designer/lighting: Baynes & Co.
Additional advice: James Patterson

A casual, contemporary hang-out, the spacious interior of Browns receives a high degree of daylight from the glazed frontage. The ground floor also benefits from cut-away elements at first-floor level which allow additional natural light in from the upper level. 'The main challenge with so much natural light was to create an atmospheric scheme for both day and night use,' says Adrian Baynes. Producing the right ambience, particularly on the first floor, involved the customisation of two fittings and the use of a more unusual source in a leisure context. Where high pressure sodium (son) is increasingly criticised in a street lighting context for its yellowish glow, here it works to great effect in bringing

The two-storey glazed frontage allows a high degree of natural light in during the day while creating greater impact for the exterior at night (above).

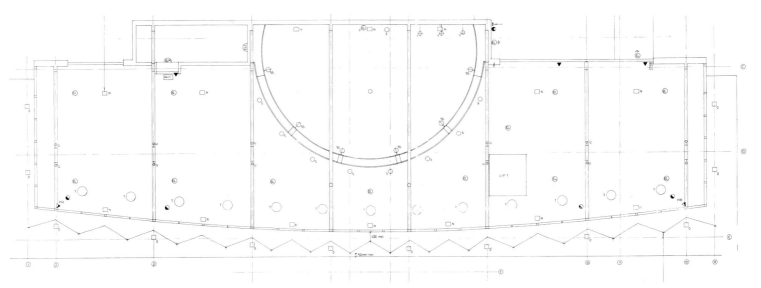

First floor

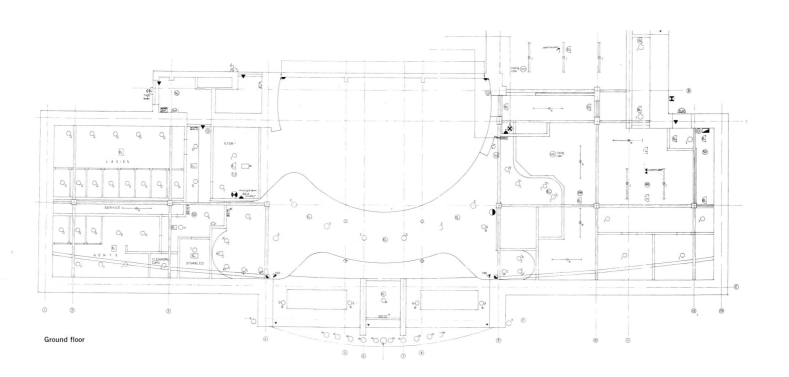

Ground floor

Unusually, on both levels, extensive use has been made of discharge sources such as the customised fluorescent fittings set into the columns on the first floor (facing).

'The main challenge with so much natural light was to create an atmospheric scheme for both day and night use.'

out the warm tones of the curved ply ceiling. Sources were housed in Holophane exterior floodlights adapted for use as uplights – the original casings were scrapped, new steel claddings were designed to the lamp and reflector units, and the control gear was installed in the ceiling void to give a smaller sized fitting.

The luminaires set into the columns on the first floor provide both ambient light and a degree of illuminance on the polished surface of the wooden ceiling. Featuring custom designed opal diffusers with decorative steel cladding, inside dimmable fluorescent lamps are warmed with coloured sleeves.

A finishing decorative touch is provided by PH5 pendants from Louis Poulsen, designed by Paul Henningsen.

Customised exterior floods with high pressure sodium sources are used to complement the honey tones of the ply ceiling (right).

Cut and Chase, Newcastle, UK
Architect/lighting: Paul Daly Design Studio

PHOTOGRAPH © DAVID STEWART

Designer Paul Daly has a reputation for rich colours. He uses lighting both as a colour element within his interiors, and to enhance other architectural features. The ambient lighting in both Chase and Cut is actually quite straightforward – low voltage, directional eyeball spots. 'I love 1970s' eyeball spots because they have a sculptural quality – they look beautiful,' says Paul Daly. The central feature of the Chase bar area – which snakes up to the mezzanine level – is the main bearing column. Above it acoustic panels were removed from a conventional suspended ceiling and replaced with purple perspex. This was then backlit with fluorescent tubes to produce a violet glow. 'Essentially it's a psychedelic version of an office ceiling,' according to Daly. Fluorescent backlighting is also used for

Throughout Cut and Chase, backlighting and uplighting are used to turn architectural elements such as stairs and ceiling panels into key decorative features (above and left).

63

'The Low yo yo and the Chromawall help create the organic, futuristic look which I'm often looking for when producing an interior.'

the stairs (20mm toughened frosted glass), while the suspended ceiling which encompasses the bar has concealed blue and purple neon running round the perimeter to wash the surrounding area. This can be switched between the two colours either manually or automatically.

Lighting frequently appears as a sculptural element. To the right of the stairs, the wall-mounted 'Temple of the Rock' features layers of yellow acrylic backlit with fluorescent. Elsewhere a pillar with plywood top and base – one of the main materials used throughout – has a backlit frosted acrylic core on a colour change cycle. The feature was designed by Jeremy Lord who also created the backlit Chromawall. The Low yo yo pendants, in vacuum-formed plastic with a

Luminaires specially designed by Paul Daly feature in both Cut – circular fluorescent downlights, (facing) – and Chase – the Low yo yo pendant, (facing, top).

small fluorescent tube mounted vertically, were designed by Paul Daly. 'The Low yo yo and the Chromawall help create the organic, futuristic look which I'm often looking for when producing an interior,' says Daly. 'I like shifting colours and form.'

Cut, in the basement space below the bar, was a more constricted space and had a much lower ceiling. Where the budget for Chase had been £70,000, the limit here was £30,000. 'We had to use a simple and effective way to illuminate the basement space, but we also had to ensure that the two areas related and fed off each other,' explains Daly.

Neon is again used to splash colour against natural finishes – recessed into the shallow step (behind mesh) leading up to the counter area and into the base of the counter itself. Set into the jarrah wood above the counter are circular fluorescent fittings designed by Paul Daly with vacuum-formed green perspex diffusers. The low ceiling in the corridor to the washrooms actually precluded using ceiling fittings. Instead, Paul Daly designed a slinky luminaire which undulates along the wall. 'I tend to create sculptural pieces everywhere,' says Daly.

Jeremy Lord's backlit Chromawall epitomises the 'shifting colours and form' which Daly likes to inject into interiors (facing).

Le Cirque 2000, New York, USA
Lighting designer: Focus Lighting
Architect: Adam Tihany International

PHOTOGRAPH © PETER PAGE (and facing)

'Imagine a beautiful Italian palazzo with a new Ferrari in the middle of it.'

The circus tent structure at the entrance (facing) and the red and white panels in the Hunt Grille (above) exemplify the overall strategy of taking the new architectural elements and using them as light sources.

The makeover of New York's landmark restaurant Le Cirque 2000 was audacious in all respects – an extraordinary millennium statement which dramatically yokes past and present, contemporary and classical and puts convention and contextualism firmly in their place. Or as Adam Tihany puts it, 'Imagine a beautiful Italian palazzo with a new Ferrari in the middle of it'.

The challenge for the lighting designer was to make sense of this conjunction. 'We had to accent the surreal interior while enhancing the existing architecture,' says Paul Gregory of Focus Lighting. 'Our solution was to use the new surreal elements as light sources, creating highlights and a lovely ambient glow without alteration to existing architecture.' Unhelpfully the building's protected status required city approval for all changes to the existing architecture and meant that no new outlets could be added to marble or decorative wood services, thus creating power restrictions. Lighting designers like to regard these obstacles positively, however. 'Working within these confines helped us to find new and creative solutions to lighting design problems,' Gregory explains.

The use of architectural elements as light sources is evident right from the start. The brightly lit circus tent structure in the entrance area conceals 24 MR16 low voltage dichroic fittings which illuminate both the tent itself and the

In the Madison Room, ambient light comes primarily from uplighters concealed behind banquettes and fluorescent backlighting of glass panels (above and facing).

mosaic vaulted ceiling. This level of integration is particularly evident in the Hunt Grille. Here red and white sandblasted glass panels (backlit with Starfire Xenoflex low voltage strip with 5W frosted xenon lamps) give an ambient glow to the entire room – and hide MR16 low voltage dichroic fittings designed to bring out the warmth of the tooled leather ceiling.

In the Gold Room Bar, four torchieres made from stainless steel and white fabric produce a warm ambient light, an apparently simple effect achieved with multiple sources. Satco 20W Ball-lites were used at the bottom of the fitting, while a 50W G6 'peanut' lamp (small low voltage tungsten halogen capsules) created a glow at the base of the inner fabric torch. In addition, 50W MR16 EXT lamps placed at the top of the outer white torch streaked light down the inner fabric torch and the same lamps with dichroic filters pointed up into the red 'flame'. The torchieres also acted as supports for two ellipses of dimmable coloured neon. Suspended above this structure, an illuminated clock slowly moves from one corner of the room to another. Sandblasted glass panels on the front of the bar and on the wall behind the bar are backlit with fibre optics – resolving depth restrictions and access issues – to create a further level of ambient light.

In the Madison Room the main sources of ambient light are uplighting on the ornate ceiling – from Lumiere 'bullets' with 50W MR16 lamps placed on weighted bases behind banquettes – and fluorescent backlighting on the sandblasted glass panels at the doorways and throughout the room. The aqua light that results from the latter complements the gold detailing which is also accented by uplighting on the marble columns. Table lighting is augmented by Tech Lighting low voltage luminaires, with Satco 50W 'peanut' lamps, attached to the banquettes and arched over the seated patrons.

Whether as an overt architectural element in its own right – the neon, the torchieres – or covert, in the sense that it is using those elements as a camouflage, it is the lighting that throughout the restaurant relates the radical to the traditional. 'It is a successful marriage of landmarked architecture and innovative interior design, held together by light,' says Paul Gregory.

Multiple sources in the torchieres produce warm ambient light in the Gold Room Bar, while sculptural neon and fibre optic backlighting add to the audacity (facing).

Planet Hollywood, Orlando, USA
Lighting designer: Focus Lighting
Architect: The Rockwell Group

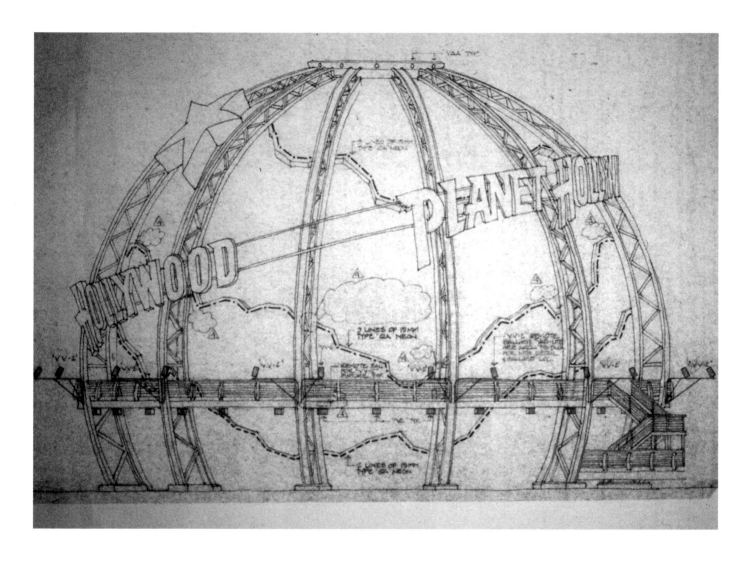

' It's like lighting a Broadway show, only more complex because people are actually going to use this space. '

The inside of Planet Hollywood is 'a study in lighting the memorabilia' (facing).

'VL' 'VL'

'VJ'

'VL' 'VL'

'VJ'

16'-0"

'VK' 1'-0" 1'-0" 'VK'

'VK' 1'-0" 'VK'

○ ELEVATION : PALM TREE UPLIGHTING AND FLOODLIGHTING FIX. LOC.
¼" = 1'-0"

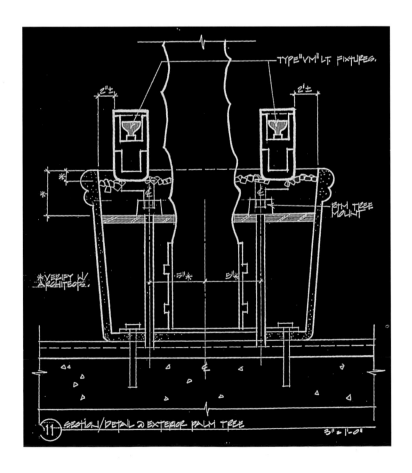

TYPE "VM" LT FIXTURES.

2"±   2'±

PLM TREE MOUNT

*VERIFY W/
ARCHITECTS.

5"*   5"*

⑪ SECTION/DETAIL @ EXTERIOR PALM TREE

3" = 1'-0"

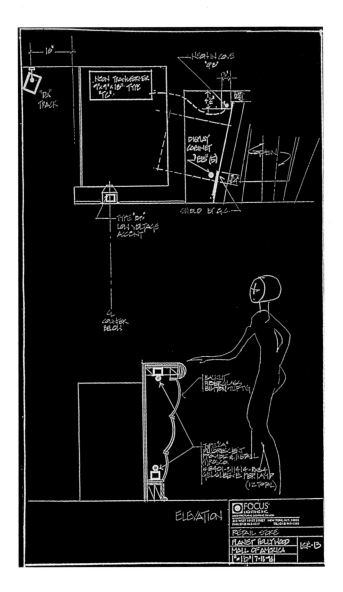

If there is a trend to minimalism at one end of the restaurant spectrum, then the Planet Hollywood chain is at the diametrically opposite point. The old adage of nothing succeeding like excess couldn't be more apt – this is the theme restaurant blasting on both barrels.

The Orlando restaurant at Walt Disney World was the first freestanding Planet Hollywood, a 120-foot diameter sphere. Focus Lighting has created the lighting schemes for the chain throughout the world. The aim, says Paul Gregory of Focus Lighting, is to give the space 'the magic and drama that is Hollywood'. Lighting the cinematic souvenirs which are central to the interior scheme is a key part of the strategy. 'The inside is a study in lighting the memorabilia,' says Gregory. Not only does it highlight the main decorative elements but also gives a sparkle to the interior space. As some of the memorabilia was positioned on site, the lighting also needed to be highly flexible.

A combination of MR16 low voltage dichroic fittings and mains voltage halogen par 36 lamps were used. Additional highlighting came from 500W theatrical framing projectors. The displays were further delineated against the bright blue sky of the dome. The simulated sky-blue ceiling was lit with 400W metal halide fixtures with blue filters, as well as blue-sleeved 40W fluorescent fittings. The aim was to 'extend the eye and create a sense of infinite space'. The clear, white light that is carefully focused on objects as diverse as the Harrier jet from *True Lies* to the black wool hat Barbra Streisand wore in *Yentl*, contrasts with and complements the direct warm lighting on the tables. This is the interior as stage set – only more difficult to light, says David Rockwell, who has designed all the Planet Hollywood interiors. 'It's like lighting a Broadway show, only more complex because people are actually going to use the space.'

LIVE! Cuisine, Ontario, Canada
Architect/designer/lighting: Kohn Shnier Architects

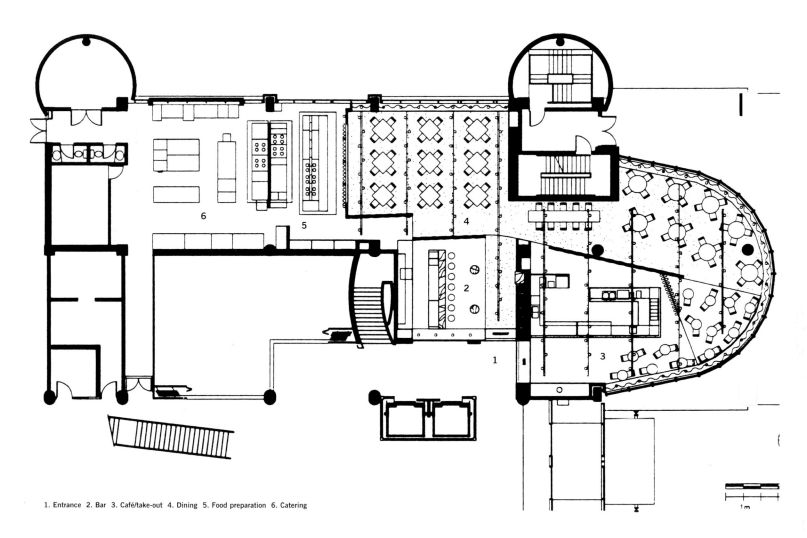

1. Entrance 2. Bar 3. Café/take-out 4. Dining 5. Food preparation 6. Catering

While lighting designers would rightly argue that the main consideration in a scheme is the effect of the lighting not the aesthetics of the luminaire, in the heavily thematic and decorative arena of bars and restaurants, the appearance of the fitting is inevitably a key ingredient. LIVE! Cuisine comprises a fine dining room, café and bar and is part of an arts centre as well as a destination restaurant in its own right.

The primary light source is an anodised aluminium track system by Lighting Services. The use of a suspended track (mains voltage par 30 lamps, ten per cent of them with a red gel) is an overt theatrical reference. Above the datum line formed by the track, electrical and mechanical services are left exposed and the concrete ceiling has been sprayed with a flat graphite paint to absorb stray light.

The use of a suspended track system is one of several theatrical metaphors throughout the restaurant (facing).

'Light sources from within these translucent, prismatic shapes make these elements appear to float in their own glow.'

Another theatrical metaphor, diaphanous floor to ceiling curtains, find expression as unusual diffusers. During the day, the profusion of sheer material, primarily white but with a dramatic splash of scarlet, diffuses the indirect natural light which enters from the floor-to-ceiling perimeter glazing. In the evening the curtains soften the artificial lighting. 'The idea that most of the elements defining the spaces of the restaurant are suspended from the ceiling is consistent with a theatrical, "back of house ambience",' says John Shnier.

There is also a high level of interaction between light and surface textures. The lighting has been purposely enhanced by the finished surface it strikes: silver leaf, white polished plaster, gossamer curtains and dark mahogany.

Like the curtains, other decorative elements have been used to modify the impact of light. A sandblasted glass entrance screen with circular motifs softens the overly bright lighting from the adjacent theatre lobby, for instance. For the transition from lobby to bar, the overall lighting level is reduced and this has resulted in perhaps the most striking lighting effect. To create general illumination for the bar area, slimline fluorescent tubes have been used inside a specially designed white onyx bar and circular drinks tables.

'Light sources from within these translucent, prismatic shapes make these elements appear to float in their own glow,' says Shnier.

Bar nil, Rome, Italy
Designer/lighting: Lazzarini Pickering Architetti

'It can be pink or blue, it can be covered in images of magnetic waves or astronomical worlds, it can become water, fire or forest.'

In repose, nil is a pristine canvas, a neutral stage set before the performance begins. 'The idea of nil is that of a blank page on which to write, spatially and graphically,' says Carl Pickering. The scheme has three main architectural elements: a continuous bench that becomes a runway (used not only for seating but also for late evening dancing), a system of electrically operated white curtains that open and close spaces and perspectives, and the bar with a suspended screen which both defines the dining space and is used for projections.

The lighting scheme is simple, with low voltage downlights delineating the space and softly scalloping the curtains which form a key element (above).

'The idea of nil is that of a blank page on which to write, spatially and graphically.'

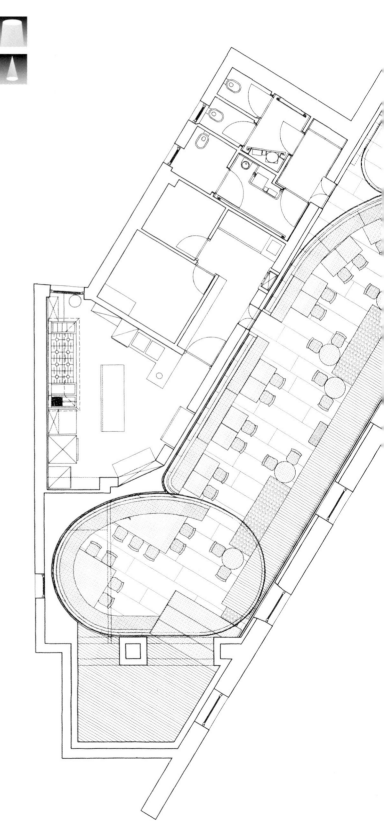

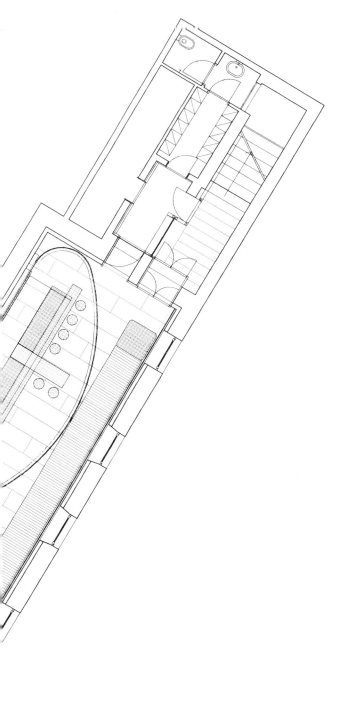

Buried floor uplights define the bar area while above them a vertically suspended screen used for projections appears to glow – the result of a 60 degree cut-off angle at the bottom and precisely positioned halogen downlighting (facing and right).

It is through the series of video projectors that the space metamorphoses in almost limitless ways – through colour, patterns, and fixed and moving images. 'It can be pink or blue, it can be covered in images of magnetic waves or astronomical worlds, it can become water, fire or forest,' says Pickering.

The lighting is simple but totally attuned to the concept. The primary fittings are low voltage (12V 20W) from Artemide, which are recessed in the ceiling, including around the perimeter where they softly scallop the curtains, and following the curves of the curtain track.

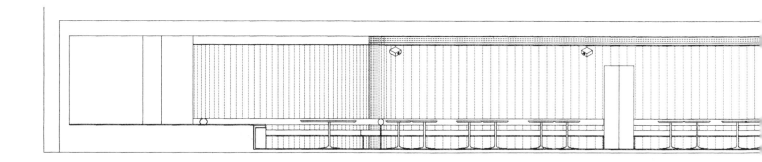

White neon concealed under the runway/bench adds visual interest and balances the element in the space (above).

Kreon buried floor uplights (50W halogen) help define the bar area, while the screen suspended vertically from the ceiling appears to glow, an effect achieved with carefully positioned halogen downlighting and a bottom edge cut off at a 60 degree angle. 'It dematerialises it,' says Pickering. White neon beneath the runway/bench lightens it in every sense and balances the overall effect.

The lighting is on a control system so that it can be dimmed according to the time of evening and atmosphere required. The system also means the halogen downlights can pulsate, highlighting different elements of the space and creating a subtle theatricality. 'Our work is always about transforming spaces,' says Pickering. 'Here the space can breathe with the light.'

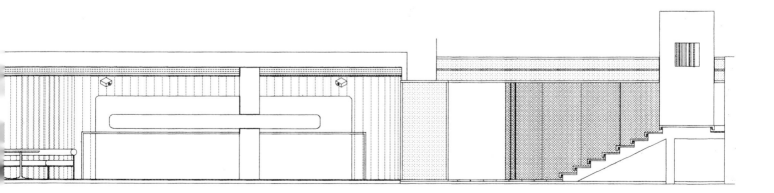

Propaganda, Hong Kong, China
Lighting design: Michael Huggins, Light Directions Limited
Design: Woods Bagot Asia

'You can create a real miniature theatre.'

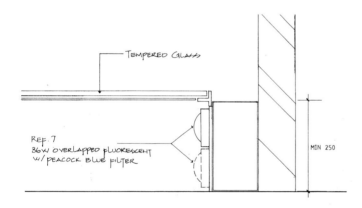

TEMPERED GLASS

REF. 7
36W OVERLAPPED FLUORESCENT
W/ PEACOCK BLUE FILTER

MIN 250

While the restaurant section of Propaganda nightclub/disco remains relatively restrained in its lighting and interior scheme, the bar and tunnel leading to it get much more into the spirit of things.

The tunnel is yet another instance of the stunning results that even straightforward lighting can achieve. The tempered glass floor is backlit using overlapping 36W fluorescent tubes with peacock-blue filters. The same principle is used elsewhere behind suspended ceiling panels and the back bar panels to create powerful glowing blocks of colour.

While the restaurant space is less flamboyant, it also features backlighting to produce a strong design element the length of the dining area. Here a conjunction of amber cold cathode and Clikstrip low voltage festoon lighting have been used behind a curved fibre-glass ceiling panel to give a warm ambient light.

'The use of toughened glass colour filters to tint the light can have spectacular results,' says Michael Huggins. 'You can create a real miniature theatre.'

The backlit tempered glass floor makes an entrance to the bar (facing).

Low voltage festoon lighting and cold cathode turns a curved fibre-glass ceiling panel into a design element (above).
Backlighting and spotlighting create dramatic contrasts in the bar (facing).

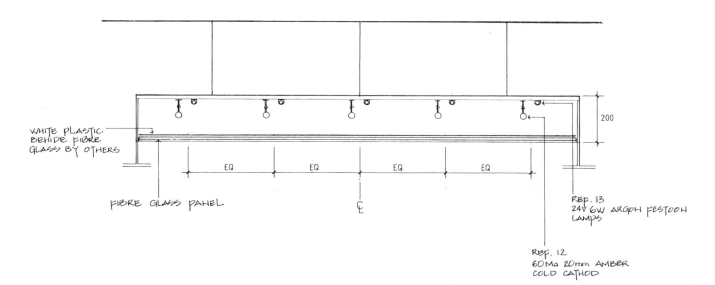

WHITE PLASTIC
BEHIDE FIBRE
GLASS BY OTHERS

200

EQ   EQ   EQ   EQ

FIBRE GLASS PANEL

REF. 13
24V 6W ARGON FESTOON
LAMPS

REF. 12
60Ma 20mm AMBER
COLD CATHOD

L'Avonture Terrace, Purmerend, The Netherlands
Lighting design: Hans Wolff & Partners
Architect: Albert Heijn Store Design
Designer: Claessens Erdmann Architects, Peter Hertogh Design

'The suggestion was to build a "cooking theatre".'

Creating an atmosphere of conviviality in the centre of a supermarket is inevitably something of a challenge, especially when the space is not defined by specific boundaries. It was also felt that this dining/coffee area, sited in the centre plaza of the Outlet for Tomorrow supermarket, should offer customers more than a conventional experience.

'Around this circle there's a shop – we had to create a different atmosphere within it,' says Gerbrand Borgdorff of Hans Wolff. 'It was quite complicated and light was a very important aspect. The suggestion was to build a "cooking

Gobo projectors and colour change luminaires were used to create a different atmosphere within the eating area and to demarcate it from the surrounding supermarket (above and facing).

theatre". The idea was that people want more than just shopping – they want entertainment.'

Hans Wolff is also a theatre consultant, a pedigree evident in both the treatment of the space and in the type of fittings specified. Featured in the centre of the ceiling (surrounded by blown-up prints of people from different cultures to reflect a world food theme) is a sky effect. This is washed in subtly changing shades of blue light from Trychroma theatrical spots, using CDM lamps rather than the more usual halogen.

Also adding colour and movement to the scene are specially designed egg-shaped glass pendants. With the same dichroic colour change system as the Trychromas, and also using a CDM lamp, they move up and down on the vertical plane, as well as having a pan tilt mechanism.

Large shopping trolleys dictated that the floor space was generous. In order to counter the effect of a yawning expanse, CCT theatre zoom spots project gobos on to the floor breaking up the space with dappled sunlight patterns. 'It gives a lively atmosphere of light and shadow – like being outside,' says Borgdorff.

Elsewhere in the food serving area, Erco Stella spots are used with white son lamps (chosen for their good colour rendering on the food) for theatrical accent lighting. Honeycomb louvres prevent glare. Small low voltage spots, also by Erco, create sparkle and accentuate decorations around the counters.

'The whole effect is theatrical but not with a huge amount of light,' says Borgdorff. 'It is not meant to be a disco. The use of colour is subtle and the movement is slow – but people can be surprised by it.'

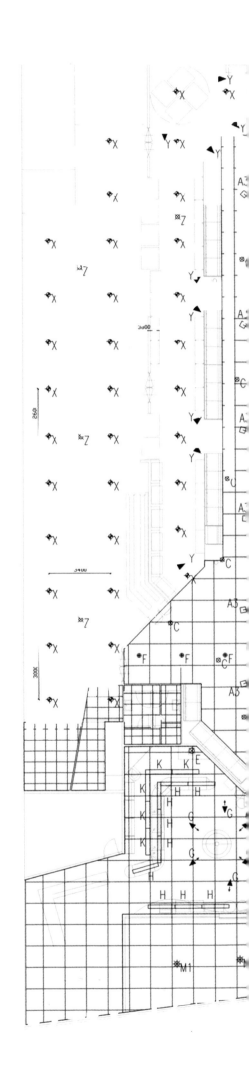

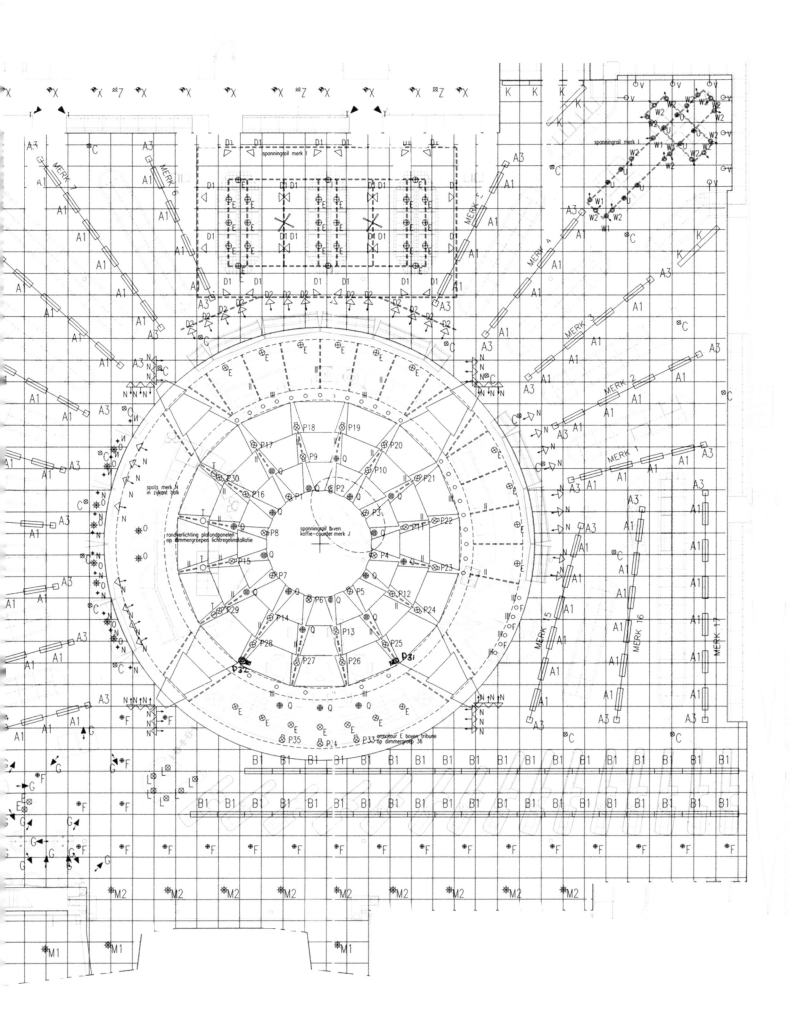

FEC II, Stuttgart, Germany
Lighting: Ulrike Brandi Licht
Architect: Buro Schwartz and Schwartz
Designer: Peter Jöhnk

'Generally we prefer not to be too baroque or too kitsch, but areas of FEC were an exception.'

FEC II is a vast leisure complex which includes shops, cinemas and theatre, as well as bars and restaurants, of which there are ten in all. In design terms, inevitably the aim was to differentiate between the various outlets, to invest each one with a particular ambience.

The Backstage restaurant is the most overtly theatrical, inspired by the musical *Beauty and the Beast* which has run at the theatre for some years. The lighting solution is appropriately gothic, but simple – reproduction chandeliers for the ceiling and floor-standing candelabra, both using incandescent sources. 'Despite the fact that it's more difficult for maintenance, for restaurants incandescent is still the best source to make people look nice,' says Ulrike Brandi. 'It's more like candlelight.'

For Le Nôtre, a more casual eaterie, the flavour was French. Traditional style acorn-shaped wall fittings, again incandescent, are the predominant luminaire with additional globe fittings on the ceiling. To lift what could have been a sombre atmosphere, neon is used in ceiling covings. Decorative pendant fittings are used to define the counter area. 'Generally we prefer not to be too baroque or too kitsch, but areas of FEC were an exception,' says Brandi. 'Normally we would also say that the light fittings are not so very important, only the effect of the light, but here they become objects.'

The Backstage (above facing) gets the classic candelabra treatment for Gothic tastes, while the cinema bar (facing below) affords a more flamboyant approach with customised uplighting.

At the bar which forms part of the entrance to the cinemas, the constraints were fewer. In what is a heavily trafficked area, essentially a lobby, the yawning space lacks the conviviality normally associated with a bar atmosphere. But the size of the area allows the lighting to be scaled up accordingly and become a feature in its own right.

Inverted floor-standing stainless steel cones, installed at an angle, serve as dramatic uplighters, while the same material is used to form wave-shaped uplighters over the individual entrances to the cinemas. Neon running just below the ceiling the full length of the space provides a colourful cinematic reference. At one end, downlights mounted low on the wall are used effectively to add both glamour and intimacy. 'The idea was to have dramatic lighting,' says Ulrike Brandi. 'We wanted it to look like stage lights in a theatre.'

A conventional approach in Le Nôtre (above facing) is lifted with neon concealed in ceiling covings. The expanse of the cinema bar (facing) allows the light fittings to be scaled up accordingly. Tight, low positioned downlighting in the cinema bar (above) recreates a footlights effect.

City Rhodes, London, UK
Lighting designer: Speirs and Major
Architect/designer: Stiff + Trevillion

'Does a Paris milliner put lace trimmings on a fur hat?'

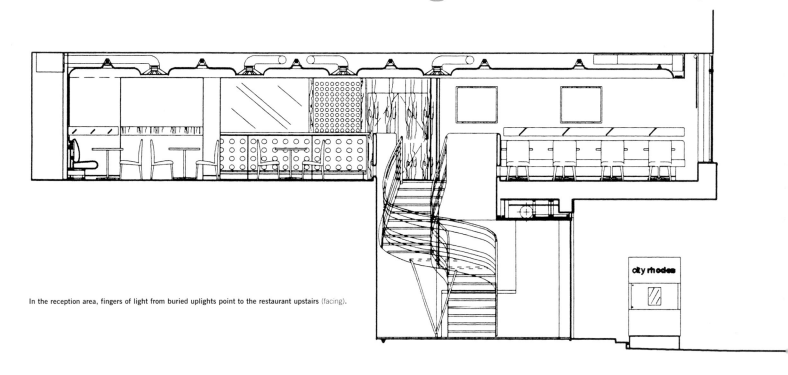

In the reception area, fingers of light from buried uplights point to the restaurant upstairs (facing).

'Does a Paris milliner put lace trimmings on a fur hat?' cookery guru Elizabeth David once asked. It is a quotation that British celebrity chef Gary Rhodes cites in one of his books and which characterises his belief in simplicity – both in the preparation of food and in the surroundings in which it is served.

City Rhodes, his newest restaurant venture and destined to be one of London's top contemporary establishments, is sited in an anonymous bush-hammered concrete building. 'Monolithic' and 'uniformly drab' was how the architect put it.
However, the unpromising context triggered an exploration of the architectural qualities of lightness and heaviness – the opening of the frontage, the structural design of the stairway that is visible from the street, the blurring of boundaries between ceiling, walls and furniture.

A simple and architecturally sympathetic lighting solution was at the core of the brief for lighting consultants Speirs and Major. 'The temptation to treat lighting as ornament has been avoided,' says Richard Blandy of Stiff + Trevillion. 'Indeed the design process began with clear concepts for lighting as part of the architecture of the space.'

To achieve that aim a number of drawbacks had to be resolved. First the brief changed during development when the restaurant switched from lunch-time-only to evening openings as well. Because the main (deep plan) eating area had no daylight to the rear of the space and the existing brown tinted windows at one end had to remain, the challenge was to balance the space for both daytime and evening use and to create a different atmosphere accordingly.

Other constraints included having the main eating area on the first floor, which meant only the ground level reception area was visible from the street. The ceiling was also low which made the space feel very horizontal. The budget was limited – £23,632 – and the programme was fast-track.

'The approach was to work with contrasting colour temperatures of white light,' says Mark Major. 'It was also agreed that all the light sources would be concealed as far as possible.'

The ground floor reception area was clearly crucial in conveying the correct image and creating an impact. The original plan was to have a row of exterior fixtures in the ground that would uplight the soffit above the entrance. In the event the recess depth was too shallow and it wasn't possible to core out the existing slab. The eventual solution was to locate a row of recessed downlights with 12V 50W tungsten halogen lamps inside, adjacent to the glazed screen. With careful positioning they lit the threshold and also threw light through the glass on to the entry steps.

In-ground uplighters (wide beam 12V 50W tungsten halogen dichroic lamps) from Light Projects not only define the curved wall behind the sculptural stainless steel staircase, but are an interesting example of the semiotic role which lighting can play – seen from the outside, the fingers of light point to the restaurant upstairs.

In the restaurant proper, a regular architectural grid of Illuma downlights lights the tables. The plaster round the fittings has been swept up to form a 'pincushion' effect so that luminaires in the middle ground and background recede from view. Mains voltage 75W tungsten halogen par 38 lamps were selected as they gave the desired spread, quantity, colour and quality of light, as well as needing no transformers. Near the window, a smaller grid of Concord Myriad 12V 50W tungsten halogen spots were used.

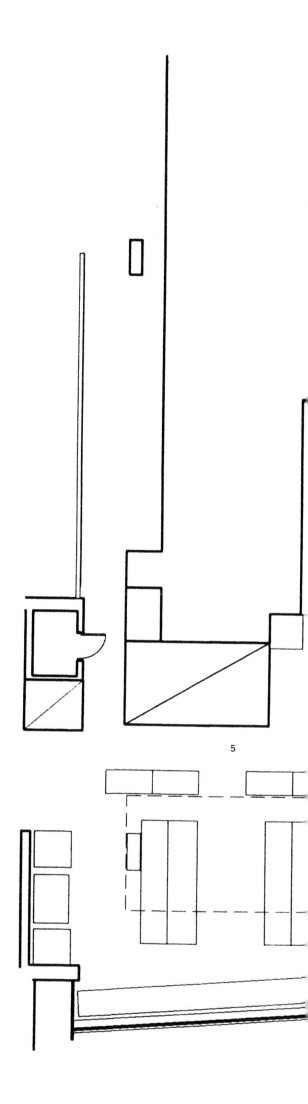

5

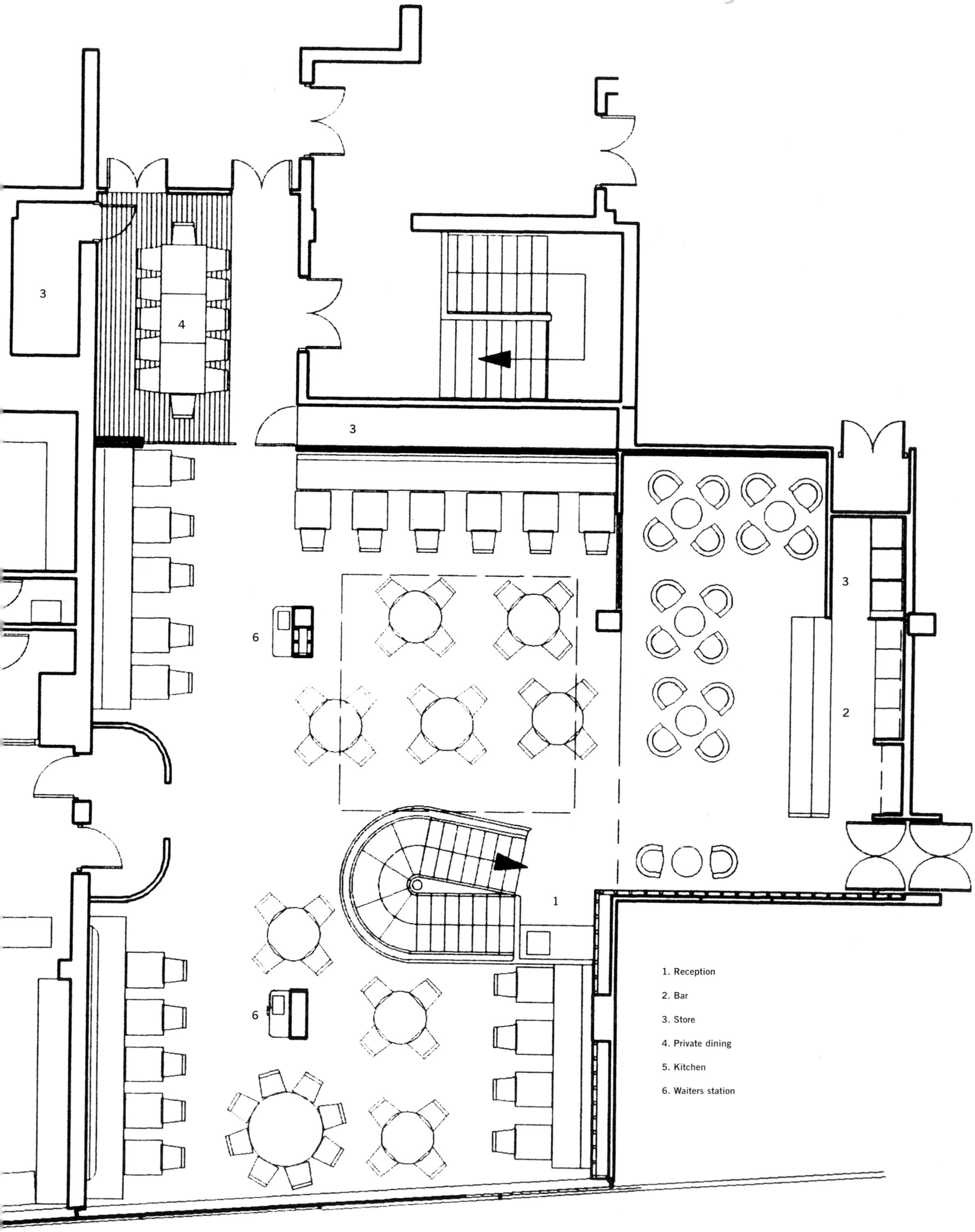

3

4

3

6

3

2

6

1

1. Reception

2. Bar

3. Store

4. Private dining

5. Kitchen

6. Waiters station

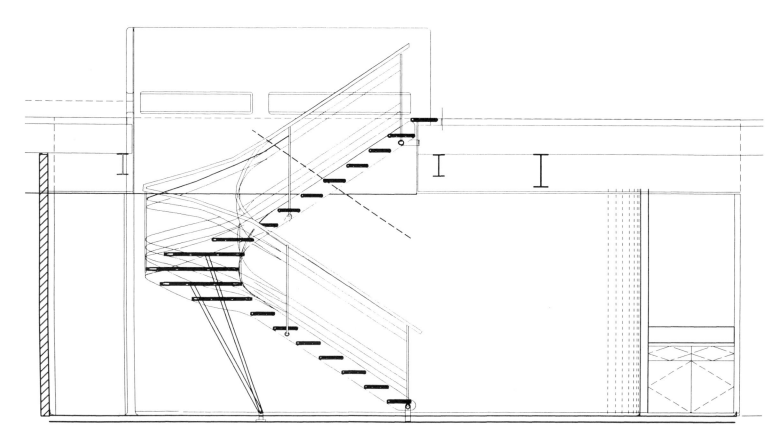

With the constraint of a first-floor location for the restaurant proper, the ground floor reception area and exterior impressions are crucial (facing above). In the bar area (above), a blue-bottle glass detail is backlit with concealed fluorescent and cold cathode washes light on to the ceiling above the seating area.

'The majority of the light sources were simple downlights using tungsten halogen reflector lamps, selected for the quality of the light they produce and their controlled beam pattern,' explains Mark Major. 'This type of light brings out the texture and colour of materials – especially food, wines, skin tones and so on – very well.'

The banquettes lining the perimeters conceal cold cathode uplighting. The curve between the junction of wall and ceiling blurs the planes when seen in the light. The illumination of the back walls and the upward-light spill balance the space, overcoming the drawback of natural light at only one end of the room. Paintings were lit with Concord Myriad recessed adjustable downlights with 12V 50W tungsten halogen lamps.

The bar area has the same fittings and lamps, again on a simple grid, washing the timber clad walls and highlighting the bar top and back of bar areas. A blue-bottle glass detail on the front of the bar is backlit with concealed fluorescent. A linear cold cathode cove system also washes light up on to the ceiling above the bar seating area. 'The uplighting, with the exception of the staircase, was specified as dimmable cold cathode,' says Major. 'The advantages are its long life – 30,000 hours – soft lighting, range of colour temperatures and the ability to locate the transformers a long distance away without loss of performance.' Each lighting element is linked to a preset dimming system, with four channels of dimming on the ground level and 24 for the first-floor restaurant area. Although linked via a data cable, they can be operated separately (from controls behind the reception desk downstairs and behind the bar and at the *maître d'* station upstairs) and can be reprogrammed simply by staff. This enables the atmosphere of the restaurant to be fine-tuned according to the time of day or evening. 'Lighting control was to prove the most important facet of this scheme,' says Major.

Catwalk Café, Edinburgh, UK
Lighting: Andy and Mike Stoane
Architect: Stoane Associates

PHOTOGRAPH © KEVIN MACLEAN (and facing)

In any context, the most successful lighting schemes – and often, therefore, the most successful interiors – are the result of the synchronicity between designer and lighting consultant from the inception of the scheme. While Mike Stoane is strictly speaking a luminaire designer and manufacturer rather than lighting consultant in the purest sense, that principle was observed with award-winning results. 'Traditional boundaries were broken in that the architect became intimately involved in both lighting design and luminaire design,' says Mike Stoane. 'Integration of the lighting with the architecture and the luminaires with the fabric of the building is a key element throughout the scheme.'

Architecturally, the project involved remodelling on two levels the strangely shaped carcass of a Georgian building. In addition to the pavement café area, a long space at ground level and a vast dark basement had to be absorbed into the concept. Visible from every space, stepped concrete ramps were used as a unifying element, not only acting as a circulation device but also as 'hang-out' areas for patrons.

Sympathy between lighting and architecture resulted in specially made ceiling panels with integral luminaires (facing) **and uplights from the floor below creating interesting effects through a part-glass floor** (above).

There is a rhythm to the lighting that reflects the juxtaposition of old and new elements within the building. The original ceilings – regarded as 'positive' elements – have surface-mounted gimbal spots with 12V 50W AR111 lamps, in both single- and four-head configurations. The 'negative' elements – the new build – have recessed downlights with MR16 50W dichroics. These literally demonstrate the level of integration between structure and lighting. Rather than being installed into the finished wall or ceiling, luminaires and transformers were inserted into specially cut panels at the workshop stage and the panels were subsequently positioned on site as a complete unit.

'It was agreed that the traditional recessed downlight arrangement, where the luminaire has a – usually unattractive – bezel to cover a roughly cut hole was to be avoided,' explains Mike Stoane. 'As birch plywood was to be used throughout, a fully adjustable downlight was developed to insert from above, thus becoming part of a ceiling/wall system.'

Colour has been kept to a minimum – green dichroics were the only non-white source and were used because of the effectiveness of green light playing on the glass and raw concrete throughout the spaces.

The budget was small (just £4,500) which inspired innovative and sometimes multiple uses for simple luminaires – a process again facilitated by a sympathy with the architecture. A part-glass floor between two levels, for instance, allows interesting effects on both levels from the downstairs uplighters. 'The spirit of each space is concerned with inherent three-dimensional characteristics – the play of natural light on white surface – as well as relationships with the ramps and with the outside world,' says Andy Stoane. 'Artificial lighting acknowledges these diversities, complementing and accentuating the spirit of each space, from the bright, busy pavement café to the intimate basement spaces.'

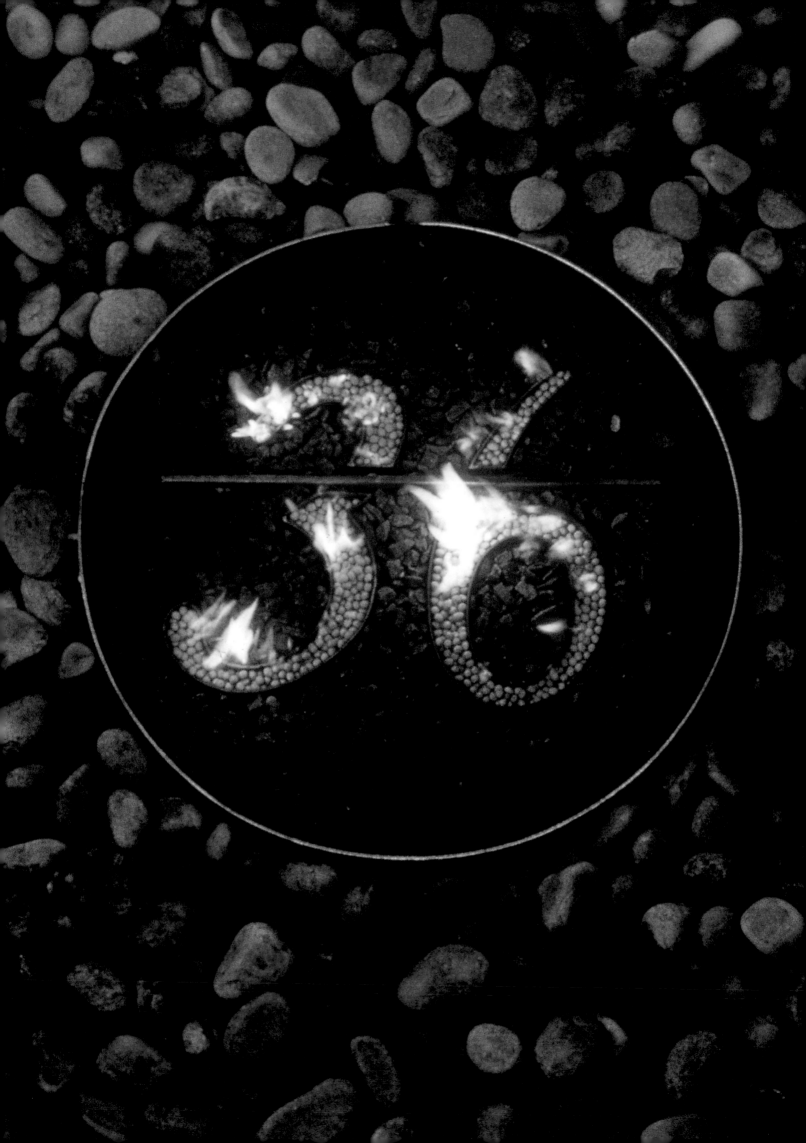

36 Restaurant, Edinburgh, Scotland, UK
Lighting design: Jonathan Speirs and Associates
Design: Tayburn McIlroy Coates

'The client felt first and foremost that they wanted lighting to play a crucial part in the image of the restaurant.'

When the Town House Company decided to redevelop and revitalise the traditional restaurant in the basement of its four star Howard Hotel, its first step was to approach not the interior designer but the lighting designer. 'The client felt first and foremost that they wanted lighting to play a crucial part in the image of the restaurant,' says Jonathan Speirs.

The area to be transformed was a long, thin, somewhat Stygian space running the length of the hotel at cellar level. The intention was to create a new contemporary venue that would compete in food and style with the best in Scotland's capital city. Where the design was concerned, that meant that the 'integration of light and the architecture became paramount' and a close relationship developed between client, TMC and JSA.

The ends of the long space, together with the panels and zones relating to the banquette seating, were developed as a series of lighting installations. While the effect is complex – 'They all play with notions of solid and void, light and dark,' says Speirs – the concept is simple. Fluorescent tubes discreetly illuminate the slots and niches in the walls, creating interesting silhouettes. Most of the sources are white light but selected slots are defined with coloured light.

Lighting and interior knit together for both day and evening settings. 'During the day, lighting works with the simple white walls to create a fresh and bright space, a huge contrast to the dark and dull interior that used to exist,' says Speirs. 'In the evening most of the slots and the downlighting are dimmed down to allow mood lighting on the tables to be entirely by candlelight.'

A further lighting element unique to the restaurant design was a dichroic filtered 'butterfly' wall light called 77 Moons. Designed by Gregory Parade from Germany, the luminaires are clipped to the wall using permanently mounted glass marbles on a short

Gas flames rise through river-washed pebbles to form one of several graphic motifs based on the restaurant's name (facing).

aluminium rod. The fitting can be fixed on to any of the grid of 5x3 marbles and diners are encouraged to move the dichroic filters around to change the colour and appearance of the wall.

Lighting also played its part in the graphic identity of the restaurant, called 36 after its address. The numeral motif appears in several guises throughout, two enhanced particularly effectively by light. Where it appears as a feature integral with the entrance area wall, the top part is backlit in blue light. Outside it forms part of a Zen Garden area in front of the entrance where the numerals are delineated with different sizes and colours of river-washed pebbles. At night, gas flames rise up through the pebbles to identify the numbers in the dark.

Fluorescent-lit niches and a specially designed 'butterfly' wall light are the two key lighting elements (facing and above left), with the tables themselves lit entirely by candles (above).

Palisade Restaurant, Seattle, USA
Lighting Designer: Ross De Alessi
Lighting Design
Architect/designer: Gary Dethlefs

'The result was to make the unwanted light reflections appear to be part of a galaxy stretching into space.'

Compromise is a word that haunts most architectural projects and invariably crops up when the budget starts to get squeezed. And as the design details get chipped away, so does the lighting concept. The Palisade Restaurant was a case in point, but one where the final outcome actually left the design team pleasantly surprised rather than suicidal.

Elliptical in shape, the restaurant is the centrepiece of a marina complex. Largely defining the lighting brief, aside from financial restraints, were the spectacular vistas of Elliott Bay and the city skyline. 'My general assignment was to design a lighting system that was invisible to the diners' eyes and didn't detract from the downtown view,' says Ross De Alessi. The original plan was therefore to have recessed directional lighting in the dining area, carefully positioned to be discreet and to avoid glare.

The budget didn't run to recessed lighting, however, and the impossibility of completely shielding the MR16 low voltage sources was acknowledged. The solution was to revise the concept and use the lamps (a total of 425, all dimmer controlled) in a random pattern, mounted on a remotely transformed miniature track. The effect is starry patterns on the ceiling. 'The result was to make the unwanted light reflections appear to be part of a galaxy stretching into the space.'

Low voltage lighting is tightly focused on table tops, while a gentle ambient light is derived from highly original chandeliers, made by local glass artist Martin Blank. They are simple arrangements of glass rocks on glass platforms, which reflect a soft, full light from the ceiling-mounted sources. 'That provides ample light to see your way around,' says De Alessi. 'This lighting was very deliberate, making the chandeliers appear to float out over Elliott Bay.'

One of a series of compromises, the bridge into the restaurant was changed from glass blocks to concrete, so the lighting switched from fibre optics to submersible uplights (facing).

One of the most striking features of the restaurant is the large pond which patrons cross over to reach the main dining area. Originally it was intended that they do so via a glass-block bridge, lit with fibre optics embedded in the grout joints. Budgetary constraints turned the glass into concrete with lilac flagstone patterns. De Alessi accordingly swapped fibre optics for Hydrel submersible fittings installed below the substituted bridge, supplemented by MR16 track heads to outline the soffit above.

Elsewhere, the real aquarium became a painted glass equivalent (numerous panes of plate glass with sections of fish painted on each plate for a three-dimensional effect), enhanced with sharp downlighting. The light zigzagging between

the panes creates an iridescent effect and the optical illusion of the fish moving.

Both Dethlefs and De Alessi agree that despite notable disappointments, such as the loss of the glass-block bridge, virtue has been made of necessity.

'It's not very often that deletions and modifications to the lighting, brought about by budget constraints, make a consultant happy,' comments De Alessi. 'This was one case, however, where design team resourcefulness made for a truly great space. It's hard to believe that the interior ever was going to be different.'

Canlis Restaurant, Seattle, USA
Lighting Designer: Ross de Alessi
Lighting Design
Architect: Jim Cutler Architects
Designer: Doug Raser

'We're trying to meld all this nice, soft quality of light, the people and the space.'

Canlis was once Seattle's most famous restaurant but was in desperate need of refurbishment when the design team arrived. Much of the old lighting was surface-mounted – tracks tacked to the side of beams – an approach which Ross De Alessi wanted to reverse. 'We aimed to miniaturise and conceal as much as possible.'

De Alessi admits that this was a difficult assignment for a number of reasons. For one thing, there were several conflicting factors which had to be resolved. While the restaurant attracts a variety of age groups, it has a particularly loyal elderly clientele. This meant that the different light patterns which a designer might normally create within the space could be problematic to ageing eyes. Sufficient light was needed to read menus and see food, but too much contrast would make this a strain.

Under the original scheme there had been very little downlighting and no directional lighting in the ceiling. This was resolved with recessed directional low voltage fittings in the ceiling (by Capri and Halo) which were focused on the table tops. This effect was then softened with additional uplighting (concealed in the wood detailing between the stone pillars) and by relamping the existing chandelier.

'What we're after is the experience of the diner and there are so many things that go into that – the appearance of people, the appearance of food, the appearance of your server,' explains De Alessi. 'So we're trying to meld all this nice, soft quality of light, the people and the space, but at the same time we're putting a fairly hard focal light on tables and stone walls. It really was a study in contrasts. Except we're trying to reduce contrasts because of the older patrons.' Not only did De Alessi have to wrestle with that paradox but also with the elements – in this case extensive stonework and potentially harsh finishes, again

Extensive stonework and hard surfaces had to be warmed and mellowed for a more intimate ambience (facing).

at odds with the lighting designer's aim of creating an intimate, mellow atmosphere. Reasonably early involvement in the project had helped where integrating fittings into the architecture was concerned, but it was not early enough to discuss materials and the way they would potentially interact with light. 'We used a lot of low voltage and quartz halogen,' says De Alessi.

The third factor was having to deal with existing fittings rather than being able to start completely from scratch. The chandelier, as mentioned, had to stay, as did the Japanese lanterns though they were also relamped with 'peanut' lamps, tiny low voltage tungsten halogen capsules. 'They were fairly horrid before and we were able to put a more efficient and softer source in them so they glowed a little more evenly and gently.'

In an interior characterised by severe lines, the Bruck Flexline track at the bottom of the stairway (and also used for the private dining room) is a welcome quirk. 'The interior designer and architect wanted a whimsical something there so rather than putting in the same old track we put in a band of that,' explains De Alessi.

Despite what must have occasionally felt like a battleground, the lighting has transformed what could have been an offputting space into a warmer more welcoming environment. 'It was a tough job,' says De Alessi. 'But the added ambient light really helps soften the room – it really was a little hard when we first went in there.'

One of the restraints for De Alessi was dealing with existing fittings – the chandelier (facing above) and Japanese lanterns (above) were both relamped for a softer, warmer effect.

SPoT Bagel Bakery, Seattle, USA
Architect/designer/lighting: Adams/ Mohler Architects

'The design is intended to reinforce SPoT Bagel's unique, off-centre identity in a way that visually challenges the customer.'

SPoT Bagel likes to create an atmosphere it describes as 'bagel theatre'. One of a chain of retail bakery/cafés, this 1,400-square-foot outlet is located in a mall. The interior is a fusion of the futuristic and the historic, says Rik Adams. 'The design is intended to reinforce SPoT Bagel's unique, off-centre identity in a way that visually challenges the customer.' Which means this was an opportunity for someone to have a lot of fun with the light fittings.

Dominating the space was an existing structural column. Bowed sheets of galvanised metal were attached to this and lit from within by continuous strip fluorescent fittings which use the reflective qualities of the metal to great effect. A continuously tapering spiral of galvanised sheet metal, suspended from the ceiling, wraps round the top of the column. Circular fluorescent fixtures were mounted on black painted fibreboard spots to provide not only ambient lighting and highlighting within the spiral, but also a clever visual pun.

Each of the six tables surrounding the column has a customised suspended light fitting, where a 1960s' icon gets the 1990s' treatment. The lower part of a lava lamp has been fitted with a galvanised sheet metal shade incorporating a tungsten halogen flood lamp which illuminates the table below. The pendants and the table-tops, sandblasted glass inscribed with the SPoT Bagel logo, 'are intended to visually "float" within the spatial influence of the column and spiral,' says Adams.

The dark walls, which feature futuristic, historic and prehistoric images, are illuminated with recessed compact fluorescent fixtures, dictated primarily by the requirements of the commercial energy code. The sales counter, menu and product display area are lit more conventionally by low voltage track.

Each of the tables surrounding the restaurant's central column has a suspended light fitting forged from the lower part of a lava lamp and a galvanised sheet metal shade (facing).

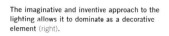

The imaginative and inventive approach to the lighting allows it to dominate as a decorative element (right).

Longshoreman's Daughter Restaurant,
Seattle, USA
Luminaire designer: Brent Markee
Designer: Adams/Mohler Architects

'The design is intended to evoke the spirit of the Northwest Longshore while revealing the underlying formal structure of the space.'

The lighting scheme for Longshoreman's Daughter probably couldn't get much simpler – it relies on a custom-designed ceiling fixture which provides indirect illumination, with additional lighting provided by incandescent pendants above the open kitchen and a generous use of table candles in the evening.

The interior of the restaurant/café, in the heart of Seattle's Fremont district, was a collaboration between the designers, artists and craftspeople of the area. 'The design is intended to evoke the spirit of the Northwest Longshore while revealing the underlying formal structure of the space,' says Rik Adams.

Industrial designer Brent Markee used largely off-the-shelf components to create his 'Calder-inspired' fittings. A spun metal dish hangs from a tubular steel pendant fixed on the ceiling. Inside are three MR16 low voltage tungsten halogen lamps which direct light upward to three elliptical painted wooden reflectors. The fittings have been mounted on the diagonal to echo the juxtaposition of two structural grids within the space, reinforced by the acid-etched steel cladding of two diagonally placed columns. 'The fixtures are a strong sculptural presence during the day,' says Adams, 'and become soft, glowing orbs of light hovering below the plane of the ceiling at night.'

In a pendant made from off-the-shelf components, light from three low voltage lamps inside a metal dish is directed upwards to three elliptical painted wooden reflectors (facing).

lightin

section three

Light is fundamental to our existence and to our perception of our world. It is a life-giving force fuelling processes such as photosynthesis that allow flora and fauna to survive and thrive. It reveals our environment to us; it warms us; it affects our mood and sense of well-being. It is a metaphor for understanding – we are enlightened – and even for divine revelation – 'we see the light'. And yet for centuries thinkers and scientists from Aristotle to Sir Isaac Newton have wrestled to understand the nature of light. 'I was so persecuted with discussions arising out of my theory of light, that I blame my own impudence for parting with so substantial a blessing to run after a shadow,' declared Newton.

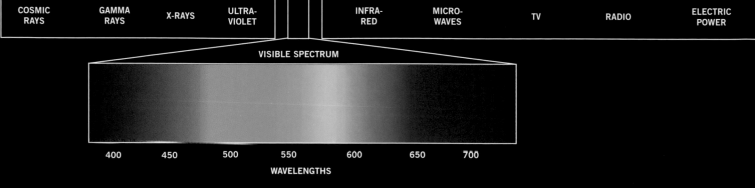

| COSMIC RAYS | GAMMA RAYS | X-RAYS | ULTRA-VIOLET | | INFRA-RED | MICRO-WAVES | TV | RADIO | ELECTRIC POWER |

VISIBLE SPECTRUM

400   450   500   550   600   650   700

WAVELENGTHS

The electromagnetic spectrum.

Light

To define it technically, light is the part of the electromagnetic spectrum which can be seen by the human eye. It is visible energy. Within that narrow band – between 400 and 800 nanometres in wavelength – the eye can distinguish a range of colours from red (the shortest wavelength) to blue. Either side of this band is infrared and ultraviolet.

The primary source of light is the sun – directly during the day and indirectly from the moon at night, supplemented by starlight. Although sunlight changes in intensity and colour depending on weather conditions and the geographical position of the observer, it is still our yardstick when it comes to judging lighting effects.

When fire was discovered, mankind stumbled across the first artificial light. Oil lamps and candles, both of which emit a redder, warmer light than the sun, were the only artificial light sources for millennia until the emergence of new techniques in the 19th century – first gas lighting and then in 1880, the electric lamp. Both Thomas Edison in the USA and Sir Joseph Swan in Britain can lay claim to developing the first incandescent electric lamp, a fact acknowledged by their subsequently founding a joint company.

Rather as horsepower persists somewhat redundantly as a unit of measurement for the combustion engine, the term foot-candle is still used in the USA as a way of measuring the power of a source to emit light.

Colour

Scientists believe that human beings can differentiate between some 40 million colours. But that conclusion is not finite in the sense that the number of colours an individual can perceive will depend on the receptivity of the rods and cones in his or her eye (rods detect the intensity of the light, while cones analyse the colour of objects into a mixture of red, yellow and blue tints).

There is also an element of subjectivity – how many people have argued over whether an object is blue or green? The picture is further complicated by social conditioning which invests certain colours with psychological effects.

The relationship between light and colour is complex and the two are inextricably intertwined. The 'white' light we perceive is in fact composed of the complete range of colours, the spectrum, as Sir Isaac Newton discovered when he passed a beam of light through a prism, and as even the non-scientific can observe in the arc of a rainbow.

The interplay of light and colour is a crucial aspect of lighting design.

Sunburst: coloured ultraviolet image of a giant eruptive solar prominence, recorded in 1973 by the crew of the Skylab space station (facing).

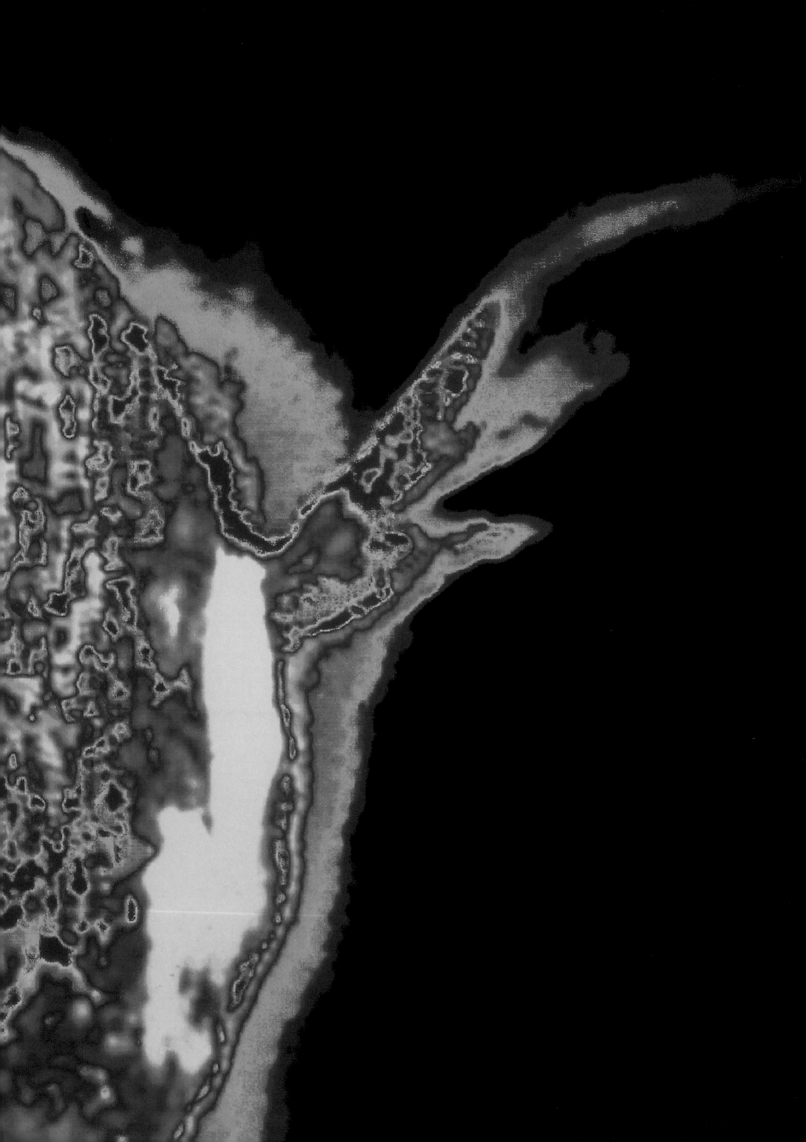

Natural light shows flowers in their most colourful beauty – as our eye would see them in nature.

Fluorescent with a high colour rendering index (CRI) shows all the colours with a slight bluish appearance.

White son (high pressure sodium) ha a strong red but appears very natura

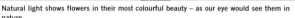

Colour rendering

When white light strikes a coloured object, the surface of the object absorbs part of the spectrum and reflects the rest according to its colour. In other words, a red object absorbs all wavelengths of light except red, which is why we see it as red in a white light. But if the original light is not colour balanced – very few light sources, natural or artificial, emit the whole range of colours in equal proportions – it will affect the perceived colour of the object.

A red object seen in a blue light appears black, for instance, because there is no red light to reflect. Or consider low pressure sodium street lighting – the yellow light is sufficient to allow parked cars to be discernible as shapes, but it is extremely difficult to determine what colour they are.

The physical quality of an object's surface is also a key factor. Different surfaces have their own colour values (the range of the spectrum they will absorb or reflect) and different reflectance values (the amount of light – whatever colour – they reflect). [See Surfaces, page 20 Section 1]. All lamps have an Ra rating to indicate their colour rendering.

Metal halide loses some appearance in red but still gives good colour rendering.

Fluorescent with a low CRI has poor colour rendering especially at the red end of the spectrum. PHOTOGRAPHS © ZUMTOBEL LIGHTING.

Colour rendering groups	Colour rendering index	Typical application
1A	Ra>90	Wherever accurate colour matching is required, e.g. colour printing inspection.
1B	90>Ra>80	Wherever accurate colour judgements are necessary or good colour rendering is required for reasons of appearance, e.g. shops. The minimum recommended for a bar/restaurant environment.
2	80<Ra<60	Wherever moderate colour rendering is required.
3	60<Ra<40	Wherever colour rendering is of little significance but marked distortion of colour is unacceptable.
4	40<Ra<20	Wherever colour rendering is of no importance at all and marked distortion of colour is acceptable.

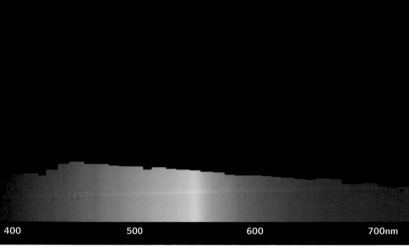

400   500   600   700nm

The spectral composition of natural daylight.

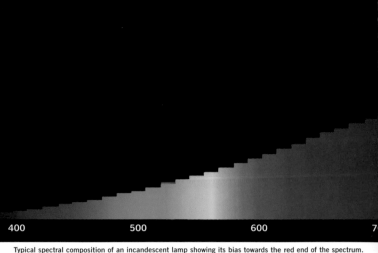

400   500   600   7(

Typical spectral composition of an incandescent lamp showing its bias towards the red end of the spectrum.

Colour temperature

While all light sources broadly speaking emit 'white light' (with the obvious exceptions such as coloured lamps), it clearly varies according to the type of lamp. The traditional incandescent lamp found in most homes creates a warm glow at the reddish end of the spectrum.

The fluorescent lamp in the office produces a cooler effect. This variance is measured in colour temperature, specifically degrees Kelvin.

If a strip of metal is heated, it first turns red, then yellow, then blue and finally blue white. Its temperature at any stage can be measured in degrees Kelvin. So 3000K is very warm (incandescent lamps are between 2600–3200K), 6000K is very cool (an overcast sky is around 6500K). Despite the psychological association of the sun with warmth, daylight is extremely cool. A cloudless summer day would have a colour temperature of 10,000K.

Any lighting scheme therefore needs to take into account the colour of surface materials and objects, their reflectance and the colour temperature of the lamps specified.

The unusual, and perhaps questionable, choice of yellowish high pressure sodium (son) for the entrance lobby of L'Odéon restaurant, London, UK (facing).

Fluorescent overhead lighting fails to flatter the vase.

A single overhead pin spot produces a degree of sparkle.

A high degree of brilliance with sparkle is achieved by combining the pin spot with an accent spot and flair beam lighting (wider symmetrical beam bordering on a flood) from behind.

Visual effect

As already discussed, the colour of the light can have a radical effect on how an object is seen. The same is also true of the spread of light and the angle at which it strikes an object. A face lit solely from above looks dramatically different from one lit from below. An object needs more than ambient lighting to realise its decorative potential. In order to flatter a face or bring out the true beauty of an object, lighting needs to be balanced.

The mask has been photographed lit by a single, very oblique spot, in each case from a different direction. The effects of the changing location of the light source range from spooky to threatening. It demonstrates that a balance between diffuse and directional lighting is the optimum solution for lighting the human face – especially when it's across the dinner table.

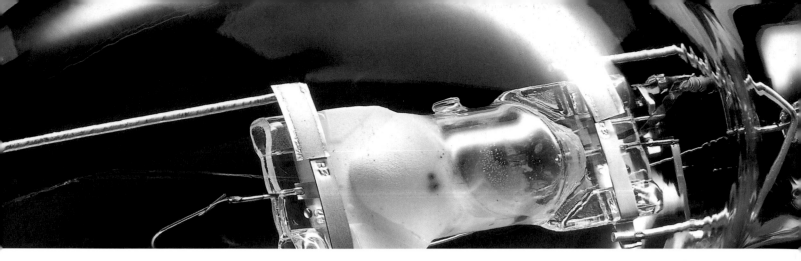

Artificial light

Selecting the appropriate equipment (lamp, fitting and, where appropriate, control gear such as a transformer), involves a number of considerations. Some are practical – light output, efficiency and cost – and some are aesthetic – light distribution, intensity and diffusion. The solution will usually involve devising a system that uses different lamps and fittings to achieve an overall effect.

Output

The amount of light emitted by a lamp is measured in lumens (Europe) or candela (USA). Typical values for different lamp types can be found in the chart on page 151. Manufacturers will supply more precise calculations.

Efficiency

This refers to the proportion of energy consumed by a lamp that is emitted as light and to its ability to maintain a consistent output. The traditional incandescent lamp, for instance, is extremely inefficient because 95 per cent of the energy it produces is given off as heat. At the end of its life it delivers only 80 per cent of its initial lumen output.

Cost

Expenditure on lighting equipment and its installation is clearly the primary consideration. However, it can be overemphasised at the expense of the second consideration of running costs – electrical consumption and maintenance. A fluorescent lamp, for example, will consume less electricity and will have a longer life if it is run by an initially more expensive high frequency electronic ballast than a cheaper conventional model. In the restaurant/bar environment, aesthetics generally rate more highly than practicality, but back of house is not necessarily the only area which could benefit from a long-term rather than short-term view.

Light distribution

It is the lamp and the fitting together which determine how light is distributed. Certain lamps will have inbuilt reflectors and diffusers, while fittings will vary in terms of lenses, reflectors and other techniques to control the direction and intensity of the output. Manufacturers' product information will usually show the distribution pattern of a particular fitting in a 'polar curve' diagram.

Intensity

The amount of light falling on a surface or an object is called illuminance and is measured in lux (lumens per square metre). While less relevant in a bar/restaurant context, there are guidelines governing desirable lux levels in different environments, some of which are linked to official regulations.

Diffusion

The overall level of lighting achieved by a scheme and easily calculated by a wide range of computer programmes.

left to right: standard mains voltage incandescent lamp with a silvered crown, PAR 20 tungsten mains voltage, PAR 30 tungsten mains voltage, halogen GZ10.

Lamps

For practical purposes lamps are grouped into three categories: incandescent, fluorescent (including compact fluorescent lamps or CFLs) and discharge, though strictly speaking fluorescent is also a form of discharge lamp.

Lamps are classified according to the electrical system used to create light – either by passing a current through a wire filament (incandescent) or through an envelope filled with reactive gas (discharge). There are thousands of different lamps – the following is an outline of key sources.

Incandescent

The progenitors of all electric lighting, these lamps work on the filament principle – an electric current causes the wire to glow, or incandesce, when it reaches a certain temperature.

• *Tungsten GLS (general lighting service) lamp:* Its 'warm' colour makes it perennially popular, especially for domestic use, despite its short life and relative inefficiency.

• *PAR lamp:* With an integral parabolic reflector, it allows far greater directional control. It also lasts about twice as long as a GLS lamp.

• *Tungsten halogen:* Introduced in the 1950s, the lamps have a light quality closer to daylight and (because of the halogen gas which inhibits deterioration of the filament) a longer life than tungsten incandescent.

Mains voltage: Available in linear and PAR versions, the most recent development is the low voltage lookalike. It has less punch but the advantage of no transformer.

Low voltage: Available in capsule and reflector versions, they offer a lot of pluses – excellent colour rendering, small lamp sizes, good beam control, long life and low operating costs. It is important, however, to have a good transformer (preferably one which compensates for voltage fluctuations) and to ensure correct installation.

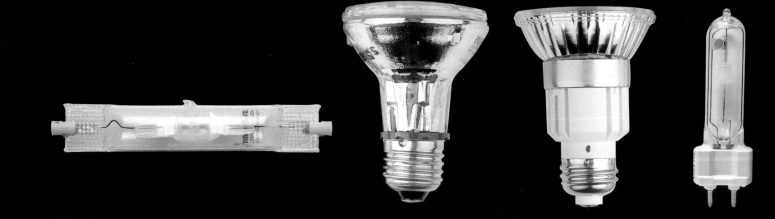

From left to right: double ended mains voltage, two types of PAR 20 halogen (electronic on the right), CDM-T Mastercolour.

Fluorescent

An electrical current passed through a gas or vapour excites mercury atoms which release ultraviolet light. A phosphor coating on the glass tube reacts to the UV radiation and fluoresces, producing visible light. In recent years, using a triple coating of phosphor (triphosphor) has improved the colour rendering of what is a highly efficient, long life source.

• *Tube:* The recent narrower tube, T5 (16mm), has spawned a range of elegant contemporary fittings. The pencil slim T2 can be used for shelf lighting. With coloured sleeves or gels, they can be a cheap but highly effective source for concealed lighting, wallwashing and backlighting.

• *Compact:* The variety of lamp shapes and sizes made possible by bending narrow fluorescent tubes has brought style to low energy in a vast range of luminaires of all types. The light intensity of the higher wattage lamps makes them ideal for illuminating large spaces.

Discharge

Developed in the 1930s and highly efficient, it is only recently that more exciting advances have been made in discharge lamps and their use become more widespread in interior applications. High intensity discharge lamps (HID) are based on sodium (orange white light) or mercury (bluish colour) vapour. All lamps require control gear.

• *Ceramic metal halide:* While conventional metal halide, based on quartz technology, has always been associated with shifts in colour temperature, the use of a ceramic arc tube solved the problem in the early 90s. The range of wattages and options on colour temperature/rendering has steadily increased and this has become an extremely popular lamp, especially for retail display.

• *Cold cathode:* Low voltage, easily dimmable and with a very long life (by the book, 45,000 hours but often 100,000 hours), cold cathode has considerable potential as a concealed or overtly decorative source.

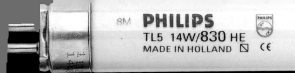

est slimline 16mm fluorescent tube.

Summary guide to main lamp types

	Type	Wattage	Life in hours	Colour temperature
Mains voltage (240 volts) tungsten	Standard GLS	25–200 watt	1,000	2,700
	General purpose incandescent with good colour reproduction.			
	Reflector lamps	25–150 watt	1,000	2,700
	Mirror reflective coating on the inside of the lamp creates directional light in an uniform beam at angles between 25 (narrow) and 80 (broad) degrees.			
	PAR 38	60–120 watt	2,000–2,500	2,700
	Controlled light dispersal (12–30 degree beam angle) with high mechanical strength.			
Mains voltage (240 volts) halogen	Capsule	75–300 watt	1,500–4,000	2,900
	Quartz halogen lamps for high output (luminous flux up to 5,000).			
	Standard halogen	75–100 watt	2,000	2,900
	Much whiter light than standard incandescent with double the lamp life.			
	Halogen PAR 20	50 watt	2,000–5,000	2,900
	Halogen PAR 30	75–100 watt	2,500	2,900
	Halogen PAR 38	75–150 watt	2,500	2,900
	Can replace standard PAR or reflector lamps with higher output halogen.			
	Double ended	150–500 watt	2,000	2,800–2,950
	Luminous flux up to 9,500 from a double-ended tube.			
	Low voltage lookalikes	40–75 watt	2,000–2,500	2,700–2,850
	Available in both aluminium reflector and dichroic versions.			
Mains voltage (240 volts) fluorescent	Tubular fluorescent	4–125 watt	6,000–20,000	2,500–6,000
	Colour temperature depends on lamp colour.			
	Triphosphor fluorescent	18–125 watt	6,000–20,000	2,700–6,500
	Triphosphor lamps are recommended for applications where accurate colour values are necessary.			
Mains voltage (240 volts) compact fluorescent	CFL retrofit	5–23 watt	6,000–12,000	2,700–4,000
	Compacts offer the advantages of tubular fluorescent in a smaller format.			
	CFL non-retrofit	5–55 watt	8,000–16,000	2,700–4,000
	These lamps require starter gear.			
Low voltage (12 volts) halogen	QT	20–100 watt	2,000–3,000	2,900
	Compact dimensions with good output and colour rendering.			
	Dichroic: open front	20–75 watt	2,000–3,000	2,900
	closed front	20–75 watt	3,000–5,000	2,900
	Well-defined beam (angles 8–60 degrees), excellent colour rendition, especially useful in food and heat sensitive contexts as 70 per cent of heat generated is radiated backwards.			
	Metal reflector	15–50 watt	2,000	2,900
	Aluminium reflector lamps with precisely directed beam (angles 6–32 degrees).			
High intensity discharge mains voltage (240 volts)	Metal halide	35 watt–2 kilowatts	5,000	3,000–5,600
	Good output with low colour rendering, require starter gear.			
	PAR 38	35–100 watt	9,000	3,000
	Metal halide lamp with PAR integral reflector.			
	SON	50 watt–1 kilowatt	12,000	1,950–2,150
	Output equivalent to standard GLS lamp.			
	CDM	35–150 watt	9,000	3,000

Luminaires

However decorative in appearance, the luminaire or light fitting is about much more than aesthetics. In fact it performs a number of functions – it enables the electrical connection to the lamp itself, it protects the lamp and it directs or diffuses the light from the lamp.

Luminaires can broadly be divided into the following categories: downlights, uplights, wall lights, spotlights, ceiling-mounted, suspended and recessed fittings. Then there are portable luminaires such as table and floor-standing lamps. However, many sophisticated fittings can be used in alternative positions and often combine categories – an up/downlight, for example.

Some fittings will take a range of lamps (supplied according to specification) and a spotlight will often accommodate lamps with different beam widths.

The restaurant/bar environment clearly offers infinite decorative possibilities and great potential for customisation.

From left to right: (above) Irideon AR5 colour-change wash luminaire (COURTESY OF ETC LTD.); Myriad miniature downlight (COURTESY OF CONCORD LIGHTING); Issimo wall light (COURTESY OF BOX PRODUCTS); Primostar low voltage spotlight (COURTESY OF LUMIANCE).

Xenon Clickstrip (COURTESY OF LUCENT LIGHTING) (above) and Vertebral wall light (facing) (COURTESY OF BOX PRODUCTS).

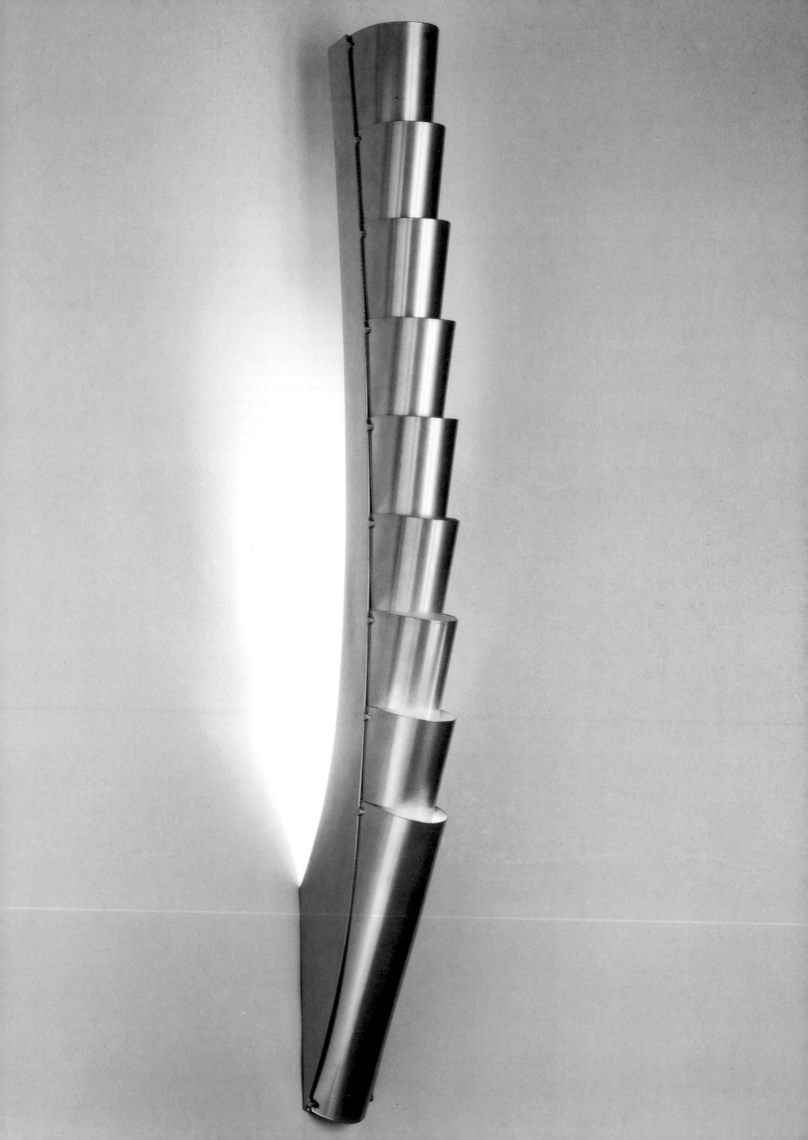

present trends
and

future

pote

section four

There was a time when lighting designers felt they were voices crying in the wilderness. While the message of the influential and integral role that light plays in any design has by no means permeated all quarters, an increasing number of designers and architects have come to appreciate its crucial place in the scheme of things.

There is also no doubt that environments such as bars and restaurants have frequently been in the vanguard of good lighting.

'Lighting is criticised far more in restaurants and people are more aware of it in that context,' says lighting designer Sally Storey. 'They are willing to accept it and actually believe it has an important role in the interior. It's therefore far less of an afterthought and becoming an integral issue in the initial planning.'

The intense competition on the bar/restaurant scene is likely to ensure that lighting standards will continue to improve and evolve. Lighting designer Dominic Meyrick believes that in future, light will be a key component in differentiating one venue from another.

'Restaurants are often still very clean, very white with low voltage downlights – there are just so many low voltage downlight restaurants. Most of them at the moment are certainly tungsten-based. The trend will be that standard sources for commercial use – fluorescent, HID – are going to start moving into the upmarket restaurant trade. These restaurants are going to have to be clever in their lighting which means using sources that are going to create more interesting effects.'

Lighting technology will certainly continue to put more and more possibilities at the designer's disposal. Fibre optics are likely to see even greater use, as are other forms of coloured and dynamic lighting. The growing trend to combine light sources with mirrors and secondary reflector systems could have applications in larger spaces.

Developers of light pipe systems – reflecting natural light from outside down a tube, on the fibre optic principle – are even now looking at the possibility of spotting restaurant tables with sunlight.

And the hotly tipped wonder source of the 21st century, the light emitting diode – offering 100,000-plus hour life, great robustness and stability, low energy consumption, dimmability and unlimited decorative potential – holds tremendous promise for leisure venues.

But however whizzy the technology gets, in the restaurant nothing is likely to eclipse the power of the oldest artificial light of all. 'Whatever happens,' says Sally Storey, 'the candle will always be with us.'

Glossary

Accent lighting: Lighting that directs visual focus to a particular object, element or space.

Adaptation: The process which takes place as the visual system adjusts itself to the brightness or the colour (chromatic adaptation) of the visual field. The term is also used, usually qualified, to denote the final stage of this process.

Ambient lighting: The general level of lighting in a space.

Apparent colour: Of a light source; subjectively the hue of the source or of a white surface illuminated by the source; the degree of warmth associated with the source colour. Lamps of low correlated colour temperatures are usually described as having a warm apparent colour, and lamps of high correlated colour temperature as having a cold apparent colour.

Average illuminance (Eave): The arithmetic mean illuminance over the specified surface.

Baffle: A device which can be attached to a fitting to shield a lamp from view, to prevent glare or to direct a beam of light.

Brightness: The subjective response to luminance in the field of view dependent upon the adaptation of the eye. Differing from luminance, which is measured by a light meter.

Candela (cd): The SI unit of luminous intensity, equal to one lumen per steradian.

Chroma: In the Munsell system, an index of saturation of colour ranging from 0 for neutral grey to 10 or over for strong colours. A low chroma implies a pastel shade.

Colour constancy: The condition resulting from the process of chromatic adaptation whereby the colour of objects is not perceived to change greatly under a wide range of lighting conditions both in terms of colour quality and luminance.

Colour rendering: A general expression for the appearance of surface colours when illuminated by light from a given source compared, consciously or unconsciously, with their appearance under light from some reference source. Good colour rendering implies similarity of appearance to that under an acceptable light source, such as daylight. Typical areas requiring good or excellent colour rendering are quality control areas and laboratories where colour evaluation takes place.

Colour temperature: How cool or warm a lamp is. Measured in degrees Kelvin.

Contrast: A term that is used subjectively and objectively. Subjectively it describes the difference in appearance of two parts of a visual field seen simultaneously or successively. The difference may be one of brightness or colour, or both. Objectively, the term expresses the luminance difference between the two parts of the field.

Dichroic mirror: Glass which has special coatings and is used as a filter that selectively reflects some wavelengths while transmitting others.

Diffuse reflection: Reflection in which the reflected light is diffused and there is no significant specular reflection, as from a matt paint.

Diffuser: A device, usually part of a light fitting, by which light is softened and scattered.

Directional lighting: Lighting designed to illuminate a task or surface predominantly from one direction.

Discharge lamp: A lamp in which the light is produced either directly or by the excitation of phosphors by an electric discharge through a gas, a metal vapour or a mixture of several gases and vapours.

Downlighter: Direct lighting luminaires from which light is emitted only within relatively small angles to the downward vertical.

Efficacy: The ratio of lumens produced to the power (watts) consumed by the lamp.

Fluorescent lamp: This category of lamps functions by converting ultraviolet energy (created by an electrical discharge in mercury vapour) into visible light through interaction with the phosphor coating of the tube.

Glare: The discomfort or impairment of vision experienced when parts of the visual field are excessively bright in relation to the general surroundings.

Hue: Colour in the sense of red, or yellow or green etc. (See also Munsell.)

Illuminance (E, units: lm/m2, lux): The luminous flux density at a surface, i.e. the luminous flux incident per unit area. This quantity was formerly known as the illumination value or illumination level. Put simply, the amount of lux falling on to a surface.

Incandescent lamp: A lamp in which light is produced by a filament heated to incandescence by the passage of an electric current.

Indirect lighting: The method by which light is reflected from, say, ceilings and walls before reaching the plane of interest.

Lamp: The source of artificial light and referred to as a bulb by the non-lighting fraternity.

Lumen (lm): The SI unit of luminous flux, used in describing a quantity of light emitted by a source or received by a surface. A small source which has a uniform luminous intensity of one candela emits a total of 4 x pi lumens in all directions and emits one lumen within a unit solid angle, i.e. 1 steradian.

Luminaire: The term used by the lighting profession to describe a light fitting.

Luminance: The amount of light coming off a surface. It depends on the reflection factor of the surface and the amount of light falling on to that surface.

Lux (lux): The SI unit of illuminance, equal to one lumen per square metre (lm/m2).

Munsell system: A system of surface colour classification using uniform colour scales of hue, value and chroma. A typical Munsell designation of a colour is 7.5 BG6/2, where 7.5 BG (blue green) is the hue reference, 6 is the value and 2 is the chroma reference number.

Optical radiation: That part of the electromagnetic spectrum from 100nm to 1nm.

Purity: A measure of the proportions of the amounts of the monochromatic and specified achromatic light stimuli that, when additively mixed, match the colour stimulus. The proportions can be measured in different ways yielding either colorimetric purity or excitation purity.

Reflectance (factor) (R, p): The ratio of the luminous flux reflected from a surface to the luminous flux incident on it. Except for matt surfaces, reflectance depends on how the surface is illuminated but especially on the direction of the incident light and its spectral distribution. The value is always less than unity and is expressed as either a decimal or as a percentage.

Saturation: The subjective estimate of the amount of pure chromatic colour present in a sample, judged in proportion to its brightness.

Spill light: The light which is cast outside the main beam, falling unwantedly on to other objects and surfaces.

Uplighter: Luminaires which direct most of the light upwards on to the ceiling or upper walls in order to illuminate the working plane by reflection.

Utilisation factor (UF): The proportion of the luminous flux emitted by the lamps which reaches the working plane.

Value: In the Munsell system, an index of the lightness of a surface ranging from 0 (black) to 10 (white). Approximately related to percentage reflectance by the relationship $R = V(V-1)$ where R is reflectance (%) and V is value.

Working plane: The horizontal, vertical, or inclined plane in which the visual task lies. If no information is available, the working plane may be considered to be horizontal and at 0.8m above the floor.

Further information

Publications

C. Gardner & B. Hannaford, *Lighting Design*, (Design Council, 1993)

T. Porter, *The Architect's Eye*, (International Thompson, 1997)

J. Turner, *Lighting, an Introduction to Light, Lighting and Light Use*, (Batsford, 1994)

J. Turner, *Designing with Light. Retail Spaces: Lighting Solutions for Shops, Malls and Markets*, (RotoVision SA, 1998)

J. Turner, *Designing with Light. Public Places: Lighting Solutions for Exhibitions, Museums and Historic Spaces*, (RotoVision SA, 1998)

Good Lighting for Restaurants and Hotels
Fordergemeinschaft Gutes Licht
Stresemannallee 19
D-6000 Frankfurt/M.70
Germany
Tel: +49 69 63 02-0
Fax:+49 69 63 02-317

Code for Interior Lighting
Chartered Institute of Building Services Engineers (CIBSE) Lighting Division
Delta House
222 Balham High Road
London SW12 9BS
UK
Tel: +44 20 8675 5211
Fax:+44 20 8675 5449

Lighting bodies

International Association of Lighting Designers
Suite 487
The Merchandise Mart
200 World Trade Center
Chicago, IL 60654
USA
Tel: +1 312 527 3677
Fax: +1 312 527 3680
E-mail: iald@iald.org
Website: www.iald.org

IALD UK
Lennox House
9 Lawford Road
Rugby
Warwickshire CV21 2DZ
UK
Tel/Fax: +44 1788 570 760
E-mail: iald@iald.org
Website: www.iald.org

European Lighting Designers Association (ELDA)
Postfach 3201
D-33262 Gutersloh
Germany
Tel: +49 5241 92900
Fax: +49 5241 92938
E-mail: via-verlag@t-online.de

Index